Air Rifle Hunting

The author and Bryn ambushing rabbits on a summer's evening.

AIR RIFLE HUNTING

JOHN DARLING

The Crowood Press

First published in 1988 by
The Crowood Press Ltd
Ramsbury, Marlborough
Wiltshire SN8 2HR

www.crowood.com

This impression 2008

British Library Cataloguing-in-Publication Data
A catalogue record for this book is available from the British Library.

ISBN 978 1 85223 063 0

Typeset by Q-set, Hucclecote

Printed and bound in Great Britain by The Cromwell Press

Contents

Introduction

Although this book has taken me just two weeks to write, it has taken more than thirty years to research. Not that I planned to write a book on airgun hunting all those years back. It's just that I've lived my life in Britain's most beautiful wild places. While out walking the hills, it was inevitable that wildlife and the whole panoply of Nature should catch my interest.

The cock pheasant exploding from the tussocks at my feet, inspiring an instant of sheer terror, taught me to see the acorns lying among the grass and coppery leaves under the old oak at the brow of the wood. Next time, when I watched the colourful feather flashes as jays screeched away into the hazels, or heard the sudden clatter of woodpigeons bursting up from foraging, I could see the logic behind their behaviour.

I was given my first air rifle – a Webley Junior – on my twelfth birthday. Thus began a hobby which has provided masses of pleasure over many years without making a discernible dent in my pocket.

At a penny a bang, every owner of an air rifle can afford to become a crack shot, capable of hitting any mark within a fifty-yard radius, swiftly and precisely, even under the roughest of weather conditions.

This is the key to hunting with an air rifle. Although they're slight of power and quiet in operation, they pack a lethal punch when skilfully used. Modern hunting rifles and sights are streets ahead of the models that were about when I started out. They are purpose-built for all those swift, precise shots. Grandpa would be amazed at what custom builders like Venom produce nowadays.

I'd like to think that my outpouring in this book will be both a pleasure and an inspiration to you. It is an attempt to give logical form to my own experiences.

I have tried to describe what has worked for me, and why. Beyond this, I offer no further defence for the book. There's a huge amount in it – I know that because my brain has now shrunk to the size of a pea and I'm fearful lest an explosive sneeze might make me swallow it.

John Darling
Seaford, Sussex

1 The Air Rifle

Airgun hunters are living in happy times. Never has there been such a range of high-quality rifles to choose from. The sport itself is fettered with few restrictions, and provided that nobody stupidly breaks the law, we're relatively free to please ourselves.

Most air rifles are sold within the legal power limit of 12 foot-pounds of muzzle energy. However, the current state of the art has been achieved through the efforts of gunsmiths and designers who are always looking for the ultimate power system. Contrary to popular belief, this isn't achieved by forcing parts to operate under extreme pressures. The idea of a rifle delivering extra power after having some python of a spring rammed down its air chamber should now, I hope, be as dead as a dodo.

Just after the trigger is squeezed, the air chamber and every other part of an air rifle become very busy for a fraction of a second. The piston comes ramming forward, blasting air through the tiny outlet port to the barrel. For a moment, pressure in the chamber can be thousands of pounds per square inch. The pellet shoots one way, the piston briefly rebounds off this lump of compressed air, then empties the chamber behind the departed pellet.

This sequence causes shock waves to travel through the rifle. Some of them are absorbed by the gun, others by the way the shooter is holding it. But they have to be absorbed, else the pellet won't fly sweetly and truly to its mark.

Air rifle shooting is not so much about power, as about accuracy. Power only allows you to extend your range. But power is all down to design: when the trigger is squeezed, the burst of action inside should happen so smoothly and fluently that the rifle will always shoot with less error than the person holding it. This is where pneumatics score over break-barrel rifles. The blast of air is available on tap and doesn't have to be compressed at the moment of firing. Pneumatics shoot with hardly any recoil for this reason.

My Customised Rifle

For me, there is only one rifle – the one I use practically all of the time. I often have a go with different ones because there are so many excellent off-the-peg models around nowadays, as well as exquisite custom jobs. However, there is no doubt in my mind that my rifle is an extension of myself. It is lying beside me on the sofa while I write this book in front of the fire. There's a raw easterly sleet-laden gale blowing outside. Not a good day for shooting at all.

My little gem is a Weihrauch HW80 which was given the once-over by Ivan Hancock and Dave Pope at Venom Arms. There isn't a great deal of the original left. They took off the beech stock it came with and fitted a lovely piece of oiled walnut. By putting more of a kink into the pistol grip, they brought the action weight closer to my shoulder, making the rifle balance better in my hands. The stock

The author's Venom-tuned Weihrauch HW80.

locks neatly between my shoulder and cheek when I'm looking through the sights. Best of all, the change from a rather crude lump of beech to a contoured piece of walnut knocked a whole pound off the overall weight.

They then cut back the barrel, fitting a neatly-tapering silencer. After that, they went to work on the insides and I was shown how the power comes from a balance between the spring-length and number of coils, the design and fit of the piston and particularly the piston washer. The lubricant, a fine molybdenum grease, adds a controlled degree of dieselling.

Finally, Dave Pope added a swept-back trigger to complement the Weihrauch's superb trigger system. With the rifle put back together again, they remounted the scope sight and fitted a recoil arrestor block behind the one-piece mount to make perfectly sure that the scope would forever remain solidly locked on to the rifle.

It was an exhilarating experience to see a rather drab duckling being changed into a beautiful swan. The rifle had been transformed into something that was me. It fitted a treat and felt like it had just grown out of my shoulder. It's a good-looker too, and that adds a huge amount to my enjoyment when using it.

I'll never forget my first trip out with it. I went out lamping one night for bunnies, but I hadn't yet reached the field I planned to work when one came running across from my left, heading for a line of bushes to my right. I swung through it, seeing it gallop in the scope, kept swinging, and squeezed when the cross-hair was several inches past it. It just tripped and rolled against a clump of grass. What a shot! It was one I had been practising for months.

Several thousand pellets have gone through that barrel since then and the rifle and I have got to know each other so well that it speaks to me. Together we have filled a log-book, in my mind, full of sight pictures that have produced kills. The loosing of a shot is instinctive now because all that subconscious experience is controlling my trigger finger, imparting the final twitch that speeds the pellet precisely to its mark.

This is why I stick to one rig for all my serious shooting. It is also why I recommend anybody to visit one of the growing number of gunsmiths who, like Ivan and Dave, know all about the mechanics of air weapons and sighting systems. Once you're set up, it's for life – or until the aesthetic appeal of a different outfit seduces you.

I must admit that I'm not very much into mechanics and oil. The fine balances that go into making a rifle shoot sweetly are subjects that I am quite happy to let float over my head. Give me the rifle and I'll finish the job – but don't expect me to design it too.

When I first started shooting air rifles, I got caught up by an interest in oils and springs and all sorts of garbage which did nothing for my rifle and less for my shooting, so planting seeds of doubt and inadequacy in my mind. All shooters must feel this in their early years while mastering the precision needed to use quite a puny weapon to accurate effect.

Thankfully, some ideas have been totally debunked since those days. One scheme, which captured several dozen pages in the airgun press, involved polishing the inside of the air chamber to a mirror-like, friction-free surface. This was supposed to make the piston whizz forward faster than ever, propelling the pellet at higher speed than before. The truth turned out to be different.

By coating the spring with fine molybdenum grease, some sprays on to the wall of the air chamber each time the rifle is fired. This coating diesels under compress-ion, and the precisely controlled explosion produces extra power. But a mirror-smooth surface is useless for holding grease, so the dieselling didn't happen like it should. These experimenters severely reduced the power of their rifles. Some meddlers do other really stupid things, like injecting special fuels into the air chamber. These explosions do nothing for accuracy so the power is quite useless. Nor do they do anything for the gun's guts. Leave all such things well alone.

Roughly once every eighteen months my travels take me to Birmingham and I call on Ivan and Dave for my rifle to have what I consider to be a regular service. First they'll test it on the chronograph. 'Well, the power is still well up,' Ivan will say, reinforcing my belief that the innards of rifles require about one per cent of the maintenance that some people think.

Then Ivan will strip it and clean every part thoroughly in solvent. The spring will be junked after close inspection to see how it has been coping with the stresses. Last time I was up there Ivan took out the piston and threw it into the workshop dustbin. 'You won't want that,' he said, 'we've changed our design since you were last up.'

When the gun has been lubricated, checked, and put back together again it will be retested on the chronograph. Then it'll be my turn to have a shot. There'll be a touch more smooth incisiveness about it. Soon after I get back home we'll be off again on a hunting trip, searching for some challenging marks.

Now let's take a closer look at hunting rifles in general and the options that are available. There are dozens of different makes on the market, and new models are being introduced each year. However, most of the full-power (12ft lb) rifles are designed to be used by fairly large adults, although some manufacturers build rifles

*Doyen of custom rifle builders, Ivan Hancock of Venom Arms tunes
the author's rifle at the company's Birmingham workshop.*

with stocks that are a bit small for a grown man.

Younger shooters have to be patient because there is no point in trying to grow into a rifle that is too big and too heavy for you, and which you can't hold properly. Much more fun will be had if you buy a smaller gun, one you can hold comfortably and shoot accurately, trading it for a bigger weapon when you're older.

Loading Systems

When you're out hunting in the countryside, you will come to appreciate that the most useful type of rifle is one that enables you to reload quickly, resulting in a greater

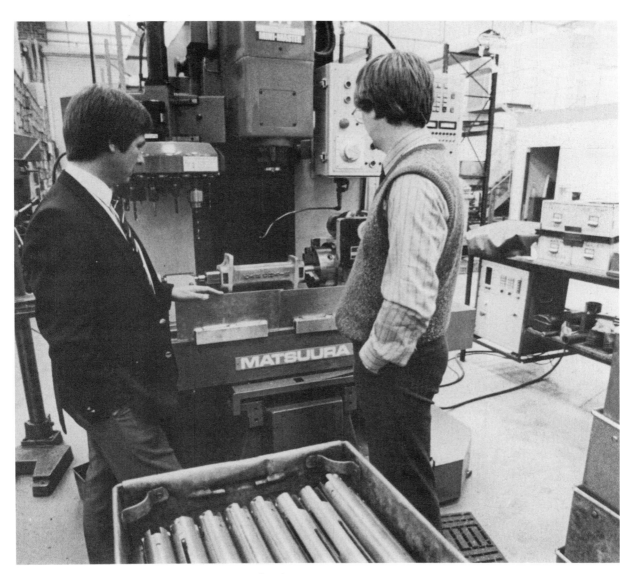

Computer-controlled machinery turns out air chambers to precise tolerances at the Air Arms factory in Sussex

percentage of game being bagged by kills with the second shot. Shot-gun shooters enjoy two barrels because they can either have two tries at the same mark, or a swift bang at two different ones, as in a left and right at a brace of grouse or woodcock. Because a silenced hunting rifle makes about as much noise as a bicycle-pump going off, wild things are frequently not spooked by a pellet buzzing under their chin. A quick reload is the nearest we'll get to a second barrel.

A break-barrel rifle can be cocked, reloaded and snapped shut in three quick movements. A recent innovation has been the development of an under-lever rifle whose breech opens on the cocking stroke – the Weihrauch 77. After missing – and that's about as inevitable as death and taxes – a quick yank on the barrel, another pellet into the spout, swing shut and you're back into action very fast. Alternatively, Air Arms of Hailsham make auto-loading side-lever rifles that are gaining quite a reputation in terms of speed and accuracy.

Fortunately the shops are full of super rifles to be yearned for. It would be pointless for me to recommend brands and model numbers because the revolution in

A customised Air Arms Shamal – one of the modern breed of recoilless pneumatic rifles.

design, and the innovative engineering that produces it, are still in full swing. The latest masterpiece may be superseded next year by another. This is important to first-time buyers. New names are coming into the industry, bringing their own brand of innovation. The best way to keep in touch with developments is to read the airgun press. There you will find reviews of practically every rifle that is on the market at any one time. However, having the latest isn't always the best option. Tried and tested technology is often hard to beat. Besides, no matter how many pounds you spend or who you pay them to, the rifle that feels best, shoots best.

Still, I can give you plenty of ideas to chew over. One of these is that pump-up rifles have no real place in the hunting field. The action of pumping can unsettle your pulse, making accuracy elusive. Not even the dimmest bunny in the world will sit it out while you're clattering away at the pump, pushing in the power. Pump-ups may be totally recoilless and capable of power well into the firearm class, but these are minor considerations now that break-barrel rifles shoot so sweetly and powerfully.

A compromise is the cartridge air rifle. Each cartridge is pumped up at home and fitted with a pellet. The operation is similar in principle to a rimfire rifle. The drawback is that you have to cart loads of bulky cartridges with you for a long day, with the added disadvantage that you need another large pocket into which to put the empties. No. The idea does not appeal to me at all. It smacks of hassle which I can avoid completely with a break-barrel rifle and a pocketful of pellets.

It is this elementary simplicity that attracted me to air rifles in the first place, and seduced me back to them even after shooting nearly every type of weapon from spud-guns to machine-guns. I can

produce practically the same effect with a silenced air rifle as with a twelve-bore, so I'm happy to trade some quarry and the rifle's unsuitability to take flying shots for a peacefulness that is kind to the countryside. Shot-guns remind me too much of a length of tube packed with nails and a stick of dynamite. This makes me consider the rifle to be a superior weapon – it's so much more subtle.

The side- or under-lever type of rifle is popular, but I feel it is no match for a break-barrel when fast reloading is required. First you cock the rifle with the lever, then open, load, and close a separate port for the pellet. No doubt there isn't much practical difference under field conditions, but the extra fiddliness must score against you from time to time, especially when your hands are cold and clumsy. Some of these lever rifles are fitted with automatic loading devices. The pellet is fed into the port from a tubular or rotating magazine. These are a good idea, even though they do nothing for the rifle's looks.

Your best bet, after making a short list of rifles that you would like to try, is to go to a major dealer to check them out. You'll only shoot well with a rifle that feels good in your hands, so it's important that you handle and fire them on the dealer's range before making your decision. Naturally, somebody will be on hand to provide answers to your questions and give you all the advice that you may not yet know you need.

You'll see quite a lot of shops with three or four dusty, uncared-for rifles in the window. You won't find many answers there – nor the latest range of designs.

Much depends on how much cash you have to spend. My recommendation would be to get the best rifle you can afford, even if that means you can't buy a scope sight at this stage. Well, the Wild West was won with iron sights, so you'll not miss out on too much enjoyment if you spend a year shooting in the same spirit as those early pioneers. Then you'll be able to save up for a really good scope and a one-piece mount to complete your outfit.

Rifle Calibre

The question of which calibre rifle to go for has provoked a flood of ink and no small degree of personal abuse over the years. This question all boils down to how much clout your rifle will deliver at the killing point. As a general rule, the less power you have available, the lighter should be your pellet. Thus a junior rifle in .177 could be quite adequate for zapping starlings, but would wound rabbits

and pigeons most cruelly. The same junior rifle in .22 would be a dead loss.

However, graphs being what they are, the cross-over point where .22 delivers more clout than .177 occurs right on the 12ft lb legal limit. So if you have a firearms certificate, a magnum air rifle in .22 would be the most potent weapon. Around the legal limit, though, there's little marked difference in performance to permit a clear choice between .177 and .22. That's why the subject is so frequently and heatedly discussed. To my mind it doesn't matter at all. What matters most is the ability of the guy holding the rifle. I've recently started a love affair with a Venom-tuned Weihrauch HW77 thumbhole stock carbine in .177. It knows what it's doing.

The problem with .177 out in the field is that the pellet tends to drill right through quarry rather than knocking it down with

The fast, flat trajectory of .177 has made it the favourite for field targets.

16

a sudden shock. This is fine if you can be sure of hitting a vital organ. However, smack a rabbit in the chest with a .177 pellet and there is a good chance the pellet will pass clean through the lungs, causing death in the long term, but allowing the bunny to escape. Smack it with a .22 in the same place and the shock would cause heart failure. When field target shooting, .177 pellets can't drill their way through metal plates and are by far the best for smacking down the targets.

One important reason for variations in performance is that different rifles produce their best power and accuracy with different weights and designs of ammunition. Thus the fast, flat trajectory of .177 can be used to greatest effect by loading a heavy pellet into the breech. With .22, the extra weight of lead has a much less flat pattern of flight, although this can be improved with a lighter pellet. An air firearm permits a heavy pellet to be propelled quite flat.

Other calibres are currently being explored. For example, .20 is a useful compromise between the two major calibres and should prove to be popular in future times; .25, however, is quite big even for a Firearms Certificate air weapon, although some of the magnums now in production would pack a mighty punch if they were designed to handle the heavier ammunition.

One point that most definitely should be made is that air pistols are totally unsuitable for hunting. They are not powerful enough and it would be most unfair to use one, even against sparrows. They don't pack enough clout. Neither, for that matter, do target rifles. These are designed to be used over short ranges against nothing tougher than a sheet of card. They have no place in the hunting field. Besides, they're pretty cumbersome.

Most modern air rifles are precision instruments; but some are more precise than others. The ones I dislike go off with a dreadful metallic clang which suggests there's clockwork inside, rather than a sweet action. These factors will become evident when you are browsing through gun shops. Even today it is still best to try several models before parting with your money. A decent airgun shop should have somewhere you can try a few shots.

Today's barrels, rifling, sights, scope rails, pistons, springs, air chambers, transfer ports, stocks and so on are of a uniformly high standard. They have to be because the market for air rifles is very competitive. The public can readily draw comparisons between one make and another. Dealers are unlikely to promote junk while there is so much well-designed and attractively-priced merchandise to choose from. We're very lucky to be so spoilt for choice.

The Trigger

Something that varies greatly from maker to maker is the trigger. The slipping of this, propelling your micro-missile to its mark, is inseparable from good shooting. The quality of the trigger mechanism can make or wreck your marksmanship. The trigger on the Weihrauch range is excellent. It is both subtle and adjustable. The worst type of trigger is the one you feel you have to bang with your finger before it grudgingly slips the piston. Some rifles have dreadfully stiff triggers which can't be adjusted. Avoid them.

On my rifle, the trigger has two positions. In the first position, I take the tension on my finger, knowing that a final twitch will smoothly slip the catch. Not that I have adjusted mine to a very fine pull, though. That is extremely dangerous. A friend once adjusted his rifle too far. We were shooting out of my living-

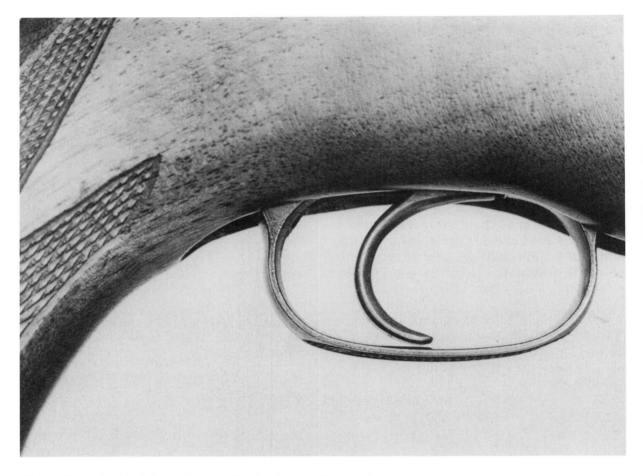

Trigger design is critical for precise co—ordination between finger and eye.

room at a target in the garden. Twice his rifle went off on its own as he closed the barrel. Twice the pellets ripped through my living-room ceiling. As with all such matters – if in doubt, get help from your gunsmith. Unless he's a cowboy it is in his own interest to keep you happy, especially if you bought the rifle from him originally. Your regular visits for advice, accessories and ammunition should be regarded as opportunities to build a relationship that will serve you well. He might even be able to explain some of the obscure points I may have made even more obscure in this book.

Handling Precautions

There are three things you must never do with an air rifle. The worst is to press the trigger while the barrel is broken. Another friend unwittingly did this to a favourite hunting rifle. The shock of the barrel hurtling shut not only bent it upwards, but smashed the pistol-grip right through and sent the tunnel foresight flying off into the bushes, never to be found. He is an engineer, so he should have known better.

Another bad practice is leaving the rifle cocked. This quickly weakens the spring because it isn't allowed to rest. It's quite permissible to walk around all day with the rifle cocked. This is what we do anyway, most of us, because we reload automatically after each shot in anticipation of the next. Damage happens when a rifle is put away cocked. This is pure negligence. Putting a rifle away *loaded* is sheer stupidity. When I pick a rifle up I have a habit, which has saved me from accidents twice so far, of pointing it at the ground or into the air and pulling the trigger a couple of times, just to check. Then I know it's safe. It's the same automatic habit as checking the gears of a car are in neutral before starting the engine.

A third thing that can damage a rifle is to fire it without a pellet in the breech.

This mainly applies to piston rifles, although the practice is certainly not recommended for any other type, either. Without a pellet to cause a cushion of compressed air to build up inside the chamber, the piston smashes into the breech with such force that it's possible to shatter the piston, the spring, and the end of the air chamber. But hopefully not all three at once.

Stock Design

Of all the advances that have enhanced airguns over the past few years, one of the most important has been that of stock

Ivan Hancock shoots an exquisite HW80 fitted with a thumbhole stock.

design. For years it seemed as though airgunners weren't considered worthy of anything other than a rather plain varnished lump of beech. Because the market for air weapons was seen to exist only among young and inexperienced shooters, gun designers made sure that the wood was thick enough to withstand abuse. After all, people do amazingly dumb things with rifles at times, using them to hack through undergrowth, for example.

A heavy lump of wood doesn't make for a very attractive stock. However, market forces have made the industry change and nowadays top-of-the-range hunting rifles come with excellent stocks, straight from the box. The custom trade produces exquisite designs, too.

The best stock is the one that enables you to hold the rifle so steady that you can freeze the cross-hair on target without so much as twitching. This may be the popular Monte Carlo design with a cheekpiece against which to push your chin, locking the rifle into your shoulder. Another design, which produces a similar effect, is the thumbhole stock. This is held with the right arm raised almost above shoulder level, forcing the cheekpiece into the side of your face for extra stability.

Length of stock is important, as it determines the distance that the heavy metal air chamber is held out from your shoulder. A hunting rifle becomes a burdensome beast when fitted with a scope, one-piece mount and silencer. The way in which your body supports that weight has a strong bearing on how well you shoot. Feelings of wrongness or fatigue interfere with accuracy.

The ideal fit allows you to see through the scope without drooping your head down on to the stock – try to keep it upright. Some people have dreadful troubles. With the rifle mounted in the right shoulder, they try to look through the sight with their left eye. Perhaps this is because the left side is the dominant part of their body. To find out whether you should shoot right or left-handed simply look up from this page and point your finger at something in the room, keeping both eyes open. Now close the left eye and, for most people, you'll find that your finger and the object are aligned with the right eye. If this isn't the case, and you haven't moved your finger, you might be best advised to shoot left-handed. Which means you'll need a left-handed weapon, because unless the stock is designed for use in the left shoulder, you'll not be able to mount it with any degree of precision.

This may mean a visit to a custom gun shop. It's something I would recommend to anybody with a serious interest in the sport and enough cash to back it up. After all, one good rifle that you know how to use under all conditions is worth a whole cabinet full of rarely-used weapons. Nowadays it's a good idea to be fitted with a rifle, as it will last you a lifetime. Within a few years you'll be able to make it sit up and talk, and you'll consider it worth every penny.

I firmly believe that if a rifle is going to be an extension of my right arm, it should be a personal weapon, right down to the action, zeroing, and the grain of the stock. Not that I'm into fine engraving and shiny wood, though. I've come to accept that chips and scratches are the best treatment my rifle will ever receive while we're out hunting. My rifle encounters barbed wire, rocks, concrete, rain, blood, battery acid, mud and heavy knocks. They're inevitable, so the best way to avoid becoming neurotic is to accept the fact.

Barrels and other metal parts can readily be re-blued unless, like me, you rather like the battle scars. They give an old warrior its status. As for the woodwork,

Field target rifles are starting to look more like match rifles than the rugged sort of bramble beaters that hunters prefer.

my advice is to get rid of any varnish or shine and oil-polish the bare wood.

Remove the stock and coat it with paint stripper. Rub it off with steel wool and all the polyurethane will be removed. Polish the bare clean wood with fine steel wool, and if it is too light, stain it. Take care that you don't round off the edges of the chequering while rubbing down, though.

Now you need a bottle of boiled linseed oil and another of white spirit. Every few days for about two weeks, apply a coating of two parts oil, one part spirit. After a few coats you can leave out the spirit. The thinning permits the oil to penetrate deep into the wood, building a firm base to the finish.

After each coat, rub the oil well in with a soft cloth. The final result depends on how much elbow-grease you put into the job. Once it's finished, you'll have a matt, flash-free stock that looks more like a regular part of the countryside than a high-gloss plastic finish. Neither does it mark to any degree, unless you actually break the wood fibres. An occasional application of oil, polished well in, restores it to its original condition.

This idea may not be applicable to your rifle – indeed, it may already have an excellent finish, especially in a world where synthetics are improving all the time. Think carefully before taking any action. If in doubt, consult a gunsmith. Finally, organise it all before you get started.

Changing Springs

Beyond adapting the finish of a stock to the shooting field, I don't hold with any sort of tinkering with rifles. I have heard too many tales of destruction and woe to recommend the practice to anybody other than an experienced engineer. People like changing their springs, though. For some, it is a panacea for inaccurate shooting.

Several makes of rifle are devils when it comes to replacing springs. But if you must get in there, remember that the spring will want to force the end off the air chamber the moment the last thread is unscrewed. A natural position to adopt is with the head above your work. If the worst happens, you'll be smacked hard on the forehead by a heavy lump of metal. There's a chance you could never wake up again.

It is unfortunate that air rifles attract tinkering. They look so simple in function. They aren't. The moment that piston comes forward, a finely-balanced sequence of events is set in motion. This has to be completely consistent. Once you adjust one factor, like spring size, you may totally wreck the action of the piston, increasing the recoil but lowering the power. Besides, designers nowadays are spending thousands of pounds and manhours in research. They tend to know best.

Maintenance

I restrict my fiddling to regular cleaning sessions. I can't see any point in doing anything to the barrel, not even to grease

the hinge, so I leave it alone. Barrels don't get dirty inside because the skirt of the next pellet will clean out any muck that the last one left behind.

Rust is the killer. It wrecked my Feinwerkbau Sport .22. This is a lovely little rifle that sits in the hands like they were designed to hold it. A friend asked me to lend it to him. Two months later I called round to his house to collect it. It was totally ruined for me. It transpired that he had been out shooting in the rain. At the end of the session he had put the soaking wet rifle back into its cheap plastic case, fastened it shut, then left it in his bedroom for seven weeks. The rust was everywhere, great orange blotches smothered the little rifle's lovely finish. It went right down the barrel, too. There's a moral here about lending rifles – even to people who swear to treat them well.

After each trip afield or period of prolonged handling, the blue steelwork will have been subjected to salts that naturally sweat from your hands. There may be smears of mud, blood, dog saliva, and rain all over it. You've got to wipe all these off before they start corroding the metal. Sometimes a soft, damp cloth is necessary to remove the grit and the worst of the filth. This is followed by a good drying with a pad of kitchen paper.

The maximum and only lubricant I ever put on my rifle is silicone oil applied with a cloth that is kept slightly damp with the stuff. Go over all the metalwork, getting into every nook and cranny. Keep it in a polythene bag so that it doesn't pick up grit and dust. Apart from the occasional wipe around the scope lenses with a twist of toilet tissue, that's the best attention I ever treat my rifle to – and all it requires. Naturally it's stored in a warm, dry corner with the scope caps on.

I wouldn't deny that there's a great deal of genuine interest in tinkering with rifles. However, these matters fall outside the scope of this volume. Besides, as research keeps throwing up innovations, the air-gun press and technical books are more suitable places to find such information. I'll close this section by asking would-be gunsmiths to use screwdrivers that fit the screws precisely. One thing that instantly causes my confidence in a rifle to falter is the sight of mutilated slots on screw heads. The scratches of bright metal show up dreadfully against the blueing.

There aren't any complicated regulations concerning storage of air rifles, unless they're firearms, In that case they are required to be locked inside a proper gun cabinet. One of these is always a good investment anyway, especially with air rifles commanding such high prices now-adays. Not only are your weapons kept away from dust and burglars, but you have peace of mind that little fingers and inquisitive tampering are unlikely, when least expected, to wreck your day – maybe your life.

Once a rifle has been set up and the scope zeroed, it becomes a precision instrument which should be cared for. A padded case is excellent for transporting it around the country. At home, my rifle is in a locked cupboard ready for use. I have discovered that visitors don't take kindly to seeing rifles leaning in corners of the house. Guns also tend to slide from their perches and crash on to the floor, which does nothing for the zeroing.

2 Ammunition

The revolution in rifle design has been matched by a similar surge forward in the manufacture of pellets. That last word is important – it just about sums up the nature of the projectile that is suitable for an air weapon. Compared to a rimfire rifle, we have scant power at our disposal – the law gives us no degree of over-kill at all, even with an air firearm. But then compressed air never will be as handy and powerful as a cartridge, packed with explosive, behind a heavy lump of lead.

The restrictions within which we operate do have certain benefits – we don't have to worry about bullets travelling a mile or more, still retaining enough energy to kill a man. Most ammunition for air rifles has become unstable by 100 yards. By 200 yards it's tumbling helplessly, and you'll have to aim 45 degrees into the air if you want a pellet to go much further than that

However, by matching the rifle and its ammunition properly from the outset, you should have no problem shooting effectively within a range of 50 yards, provided you are selective with your targets. This point is fundamental to rifle hunting. Look at it this way. You send a tiny lump of lead whizzing at high speed towards your quarry, intending that it should cause lethal destruction when it arrives.

A few yards out, the initial surge of power is being slowed by gravity, friction with the atmosphere, and air turbulence. The rifling inside the barrel spun the pellet before it emerged, helping it to drill through the air without loss of stability. But it's quite a feeble projectile and soon it's slowing rapidly, angling more and more steeply towards the ground. A strong side wind would curve it further to one side of your line of sight.

Much depends on your degree of accuracy and the power of your outfit, but most standard rifles will hit a rabbit effectively, in the head, at up to 40 yards. At 60 yards, there's barely enough energy left in the pellet to knock down a starling.

Because air weapons are somewhat puny, you have to make sure that you can see your quarry well enough to be able to aim and shoot at its head, neck, or heart – never the body because it contains no vital organs which, when damaged, cause instant death. You may notice that I am not coy about such matters, unlike the politician I met while photographing a driven pheasant shoot for a magazine. 'Please don't take my picture,' said he. 'All of my constituents are animal-lovers.'

I decided long ago that sex and hunting are the oldest of instincts. When they manage to ban the former, I'll agree to them suppressing the latter. I have spent all my life studying birds, animals and fish, and as Nature decrees that hunting is respectable for them, I see no reason why I should deny an instinct which has brought my species, *Homo sapiens*, from the plains to world domination through five million years of evolution. Man never got anywhere by denying Nature.

Pellet Design

We hunters, then, have to be scientific

about the effect we produce with that tiny pellet. It has to arrive precisely at the right place, smashing its way through flesh and bone, with enough energy left to produce a lethal shock. It doesn't necessarily happen that the two go together. Some pellets aren't suitable. They drill their way through, producing scant shock wave in front, and very little hydraulic shock as the flesh is sucked in behind. If the skin on the other side doesn't billow and stop them, they'll pass right through without stopping.

It is always wise, especially in the early days, to check how the pellet performed. You have only to remember how your quarry was standing when you fired, then check to see if there's an exit hole as well as an entry hole. Small animals are likely to be drilled, anyway, no matter what the ammunition. Very often a head-shot at a rabbit from short range will produce a ricochet as the pellet whines off the hard earth behind, with the rabbit slumping stone dead in the grass.

Some designs are worse than others. Quite a lot of .177 ammunition is suspect, as are some designs of steel pellets inside plastic jackets. Pointed designs, in any calibre, are inconsistent. Much depends on your own outfit, but for all my shooting I use the flat-head diabolo design. This is very accurate in flight and when it hits home it transfers all its remaining energy into brutalising the target zone. It kills cleanly.

A recent advance on this has been a slightly recessed flat nose, using the dum-dum principle. This assists the pellet to spread and deform on impact, stopping it from simply drilling its way through, but producing great shock instead.

Pellet design is quite complicated. Basically there are three parts to a pellet – the head, waist, and skirt. The head is intended to touch the ridges of the rifling all round the barrel. It also requires a certain mass of lead to keep its shape when it penetrates rather than blow into little fragments. It must also be of a uniform shape and density, else the atmosphere will deflect it from its path. This last factor particularly affects pointed pellets. Minor damage to the point causes them to stray.

The waist reduces the area of contact between pellet and barrel, minimising friction. It probably produces extra stability by emphasising the centrifugal force in the pellet's head and skirt after being spun by the rifling. The skirt also plays another very important role.

When you pull the trigger, the blast of air bangs the pellet from behind, which forces the skirt to spread out and grip the rifling as it squeezes from the breech and into the barrel. This seals the air behind the pellet and causes it to linger long enough for pressure to increase before it zings along the barrel.

The standard round-headed pellet is a design which has stood the tests of time and which has served me well over the years. There are many different makes and weights available nowadays, and most of them are suitable for hunting.

Most designs of rifle will work best with only a few different brands of pellet. Many of these combinations are common knowledge nowadays, so your dealer will be able to help you out. Contrary to what you might be led to believe from all those charts you sometimes see comparing different makes of pellet in a specific rifle, the nitty-gritty isn't the final foot-ounce of power you can get, but the degree of accuracy with which you bang a pellet into the bull.

In the final analysis, there are several brands of pellet with little difference in performance to choose between them. Because consistent accuracy with your favourite rifle is the purpose behind a great deal of your shooting, other considerations come in to the equation when you buy ammo.

One of these is supply. Dealers prefer to stock popular brands. It is sensible to choose one that, despite the occasional slight variation in weight and size between batches, will be as widely available in five years as it is today. There is no point in buying job lots – even for practice shots. They're reduced to clear because they perform badly. This means that you won't learn a great deal about your outfit's performance for as long as you use them. A major attraction of airgunning is the fact that ammo is so cheap, permitting plenty of inexpensive shooting. Even so, it is probably best to regard each shot, apart from warm-ups, as a serious event.

I once bought a job lot. They were very crudely made. Practically all pellets are stamped by machine out of lead wire, but these must have been made with a prototype stamp. They were the familiar round–headed type, except that the round heads varied greatly in roundness and width. They weighed more or less the same, but that was about it. Sometimes it was almost impossible to force a pellet into the breech, while others slipped half an inch up the barrel. I gave away boxes of them to people who wanted only to mess around with a rifle rather than to shoot seriously.

Because the performance of a pellet is controlled by the fine balances between the air blast and the breech, barrel and pellet designs, it is possible to spend hours testing different brands. I prefer to spend that time out in the woods and fields. My favourite .22 ammunition is fairly heavy so I have to keep an eye on its trajectory if long-range shots are to produce kills. However, I'm happy that the rifle produces its maximum muzzle energy with this pellet, ensuring the flattest possible trajectory for the heftiest missile my gun can handle.

Being lighter, a .177 pellet naturally has a flatter trajectory, but I'm not so impressed by the degree of demolition that takes place when it arrives. On the other hand, you can buy or mould solid spitzer bullets to fire through your rifle. These really do have a lumpy trajectory, and don't produce any more game in the bag as a result of the extra weight and clout. Range is reduced, so is precision, even in an air firearm.

You should be aware that there are two sizes of .22 – German and British. The European calibre is a fraction smaller, making their ammunition fit loosely in British rifles, while British ammo fits German rifles tightly.

Other Ammunition

Never use darts in a decent rifle. The plastic ones are a dead loss because they fly anywhere they like and can leave smears of plastic inside the barrel which are hard to get off. Metal darts should be avoided, too, but for a different reason. They can damage the rifling and scratch the inside of the barrel. Neither of these effects does anything for the consistent performance of a rifle, nor do the projectiles have any relevance to the hunting field.

In recent years there has been what strikes me as an attempt to convert .22 rifles to .177. This isn't really the case, although it is tantamount to the effect produced by fitting a metal pellet with a plastic sheath. In one design the sheath flies clear after leaving the barrel. Another type permits the complete projectile to reach its target, with the plastic separating away as it penetrates, letting the metal part drill on through.

Despite extensive advertising which has undoubtedly boosted interest and therefore sales, I can't see any use for them.

The pellet on the left was fired into a barrel of water – that on the right is straight from the tin. Both are .22 RWS Diabolo. The right one shows a seam and flakes of swarf left by machining. The left one shows where the air blast has pushed the skirt into the rifling, which has gripped the head lightly, leaving tiny notches on top and at left. On impact, even with water, the flat head forced the pellet to slow rapidly, mushroom, increase in diameter, and even to crack around the end. This picture demonstrates that lead is best for translating air speed into lethal shocking energy.

Nobody has yet convinced me that they add anything to a hunting trip. Lead is traditional, and out there absolutely nothing will ever beat a well-designed lead pellet. You have only to tip some out of the tin and into your pocket to be ready for action.

Some plastic-skirted pellets are unsuitable for use in an FAC air weapon because they may separate inside the barrel. I once watched a friend testing a batch. They become unstable in flight within yards of the muzzle. The same also applies to several makes of lead pellet when they're used in air firearms. These tend to be the lighter designs, without the mass to carry the power that the rifle loads them with. Six inch groups at twenty yards are what you'll see if this happens, with some pellets straying completely off target.

Anybody who buys an air firearm is advised to stick rigidly to the brand of ammo that the maker recommends. These rifles generate pressures that need to be used and controlled by the pellet. Ammunition that works well in a standard rifle may be so unsuited to a firearm that it damages the rifle's innards. One sure sign that all's not well is the piston recocking itself after a shot. This is caused by the piston coming forward too fast and bouncing all the way back, re-engaging the trigger. The problem is readily avoided by tempering power with a heavier projectile.

Testing Muzzle Energy

It is very easy, especially during the early days of being an inaccurate hopeful, to feel that your rifle is too puny for effective hunting. In some cases this may be so, but it's a widespread neurosis that affects us all from time to time – especially after a session when nothing seemed willing to drop down dead. Assuming that your outfit is in good mechanical condition and suited to your ammunition, you can check this by obtaining a chronograph.

This consists of two electronic eyes which measure the speed at which the pellet passes between them. With a formula, you multiply the speed by the pellet's weight and arrive at your muzzle energy. This is the best way to find how different pellets perform in your rifle. It also permits you, when a mate claims that his rifle can shoot right through a dustbin, to be more responsible and discover by scientific means whether yours would do the same. This is bound to happen because once your friends learn that you have a chrono-

graph, they'll want you to test their rifles for them. Comparisons, however, are only valid if shooting conditions remain the same. For example, a rifle that has been left in the sun will become so hot that the lubricant will creep into the air chamber more readily. This increases the dieselling effect (adding nothing to accuracy), and produces misleading readings.

There is a simple formula for getting sense from a chronograph. Find the muzzle velocity from the machine in feet per second (fps). Say this is 600fps. Now square this figure (360,000). Multiply this by the pellet's weight, in grains (say 14.5 grains for Eley Wasp). The figure is now 5,220,000. Divide this by 450240 (the common factor), and you arrive at a figure of 11.59 – the muzzle energy in ft lb with Eley Wasp in your rifle.

Another alternative to dustbins, tin cans, planks and telephone directories is ballistic putty. This is stiffer than normal putty and Plasticine so you don't need so much to stop a pellet passing right through. After each shot, take a knife and cut along the hole left by the pellet. You'll be able to measure how suitable it is for hunting. With practice, you'll be able to interpret from the nature of the hole (whether torn or smooth-sided) how well a pellet combines penetration with energy dissipation through shock. After all, a pellet which drills itself far into the putty may not be very good at knocking down game.

As with all such matters, scientific understanding goes only part of the way. Theory frequently contradicts experience. Whatever brands of rifle and ammo you finally end up with, you'll have more fun and become an even hotter shot if you attach most importance to their ultimate effect. Therefore, as this book is about hunting with air rifles, the main criterion must be how much game ends up in the larder.

Sizing and Carrying

Nowadays you can buy little ammunition clips to stick or screw to the off side of the stock. These hold pellets firmly and ready to hand. However, they really do intrude on the aesthetic lines of a rifle. Neither do they increase speed of reloading, because it will always be just as quick to dip your fingers into your pocket when the next pellet is required. It should be a clean pocket, though – not full of fluff, grit and bits of sticks.

You can also buy little gadgets which ensure that each pellet is of identical size. This is probably most critical for field target shooters. Size determines friction as the pellet travels up the barrel, and this is an important part of the search for ultimate consistency of performance. Weight is just as critical, too. Many top field target shooters buy large batches of pellets and weigh every one, discarding maybe half the batch because they fall above or below the ideal weight. This means buying a highly accurate set of scales, and they're not cheap, especially to detect differences in fractions of a grain.

Nevertheless, I have to admit that all this scarcely interests me, although it undoubtedly applies to the exacting world of field target shooting. To my mind, such tiny factors are drowned out by all the other ones that are present on a hunting trip. There's more to consistent shooting than weights and measures.

3 Sights

Telescopic sights have become so popular on air rifles in recent times that some new models come without iron sights fixed to them. It is certainly true that a scope will make a good shot better and can even make a poor shot more aware of those areas of his technique that need brushing up. However, one of the most accurate rifles I've ever handled was fitted with iron sights. It was a very rare Winchester 'One of One Thousand' – a super-accurate version of the famous gun that tamed the West.

It has to be admitted that the general standard of iron sights – also known as open sights – that come fitted to air rifles is sometimes not as high as it should be. They lack the precision that you find on even a mass-produced rifle like the Lee-Enfield, millions of which were made in the last war. Although many air rifles shoot quite accurately with open sights, I rarely feel as though my adjustments are as precise as I'd like them to be. Having said this, I allow that some manufacturers, like good old Webley, produce a fair open sight.

The front sight that is currently fashionable is the tunnel version. Some come with interchangeable elements. You unscrew a knurled knob at the back and slip in a different style of front element. The trouble is that there's quite a lot of side to side play with these elements, so you have to reset the back sight to compensate. Another problem is that the knurled knob can work loose, slackening its hold on the element. When this happens, your point of zero is ruined. The way to minimise this hassle is to make sure that when you screw up tight, you push the element as far as it will go to one side. At least it will be consistent.

You only need one element – a chisel tapering to a fine flat tip. That's best for hunting. In the old days you could buy a rifle with such a sight fitted, without the hood. It would be about half an inch long, a solid blade of steel that would withstand any knock or bang – unlike tunnel foresights which reach out for obstacles. The solid blade would also be tapered towards the shooter, the edge blued to a dull dark finish. If dark quarry was against a dim background, you could dab that wee ramp with a drip of saliva for it to turn white with reflected sky. Clever, those old-timers.

It is ironic, now that scopes are so popular, that tunnel foresights should become so widespread. The moment you fit a scope to a rifle, nowadays, you find a dark blur at the bottom of the sight picture. Soon you are hunting for a screwdriver to remove the thing. Even when they're gone, tunnel foresights are an eyesore, leaving a gaping gash along both sides of the muzzle. They really are an ugly appendage to a rifle. One practical virtue is that they anchor the adaptor which some rifles require before a silencer can be fitted.

Open Sights

I suppose that scopes have made iron sights something of an anachronism. I find this sad. However, if a neat ramp foresight had been fitted to my HW80, it would have gone into the dustbin after Venom Arms cut back the barrel and fitted that slinky, taper-fit silencer. Still, it's good to be like the old pioneers from time to time and shoot with open sights. The sound of the rear sight clicking and the feel of oil on the fingers after each adjustment, not to mention its smell, must bring back memories to older shooters. For windage and elevation adjustment – horizontal and vertical hold – simply move the notch in the rear sight to the left to hit further left, and up to hit higher. Those were the days. The trouble is, you don't get many good rear-sights, either, nowadays. The notch itself should be as clean-cut as though a scalpel took it out. To make it stand out clearly, even when slightly out of focus, it should be black and so matt that not a gleam comes from it.

Open sights allow you to shoot more quickly because your brain doesn't have to adjust to a different view when the scope comes to your eye. Neither do you have to aim too precisely after a while. If your rifle fits and you have shot together for a few years, the rear and front sights will automatically align as you mount the rifle. You have only to set the foresight on your mark for a swift kill.

But iron sights are useless for lamping, especially with a lamp mounted on your forehead. It will flood the sights with so much light that you'll not be able to make out anything beyond them. Even a lamp held by somebody else is little better because, for use in low light conditions, most open sights on air weapons lack that definitive edge of precision.

Scope Sights

Only a scope will allow you to develop precision and accuracy to their ultimate level. But there are scopes and scopes. Leave on the dealer's shelf those tinny Oriental jobs that look like long black cigars with feeble built-on mounts. They don't let much light through and they're readily jarred off zero – assuming they let you achieve this in the first place. A bad scope is vastly inferior to open sights, and a good scope is as precise an instrument as a hunting rifle.

I'll go through the various parts of my own scope, itemising the good points, the less good ones, and other factors to be borne in mind when making a selection. Mine is an Optima Moonlighter, 3 – 9 × 56. This means that it has variable magnification between 3 and 9 times the size of the object as seen by the naked eye. I don't use the variable adjustment but keep it fixed on six power. Photographers among you will recognise this as the equivalent of a 300mm lens in 35mm format.

This is quite some magnification. I have used less powerful scopes in the past, but find that six power allows me to be that little bit more precise. It is also the upper limit before things start going out of focus. The nine power scope has a narrow depth of focus, making it difficult to find both target and cross-hairs at some ranges.

I once read somewhere that too powerful a scope will make you feel you're trying to hold steady in a rough sea. In other words, your shakes will be magnified too, and that's a bad thing. Well, my opinion differs. Only by being critically aware of the degree to which you wobble on target will you care enough to improve. There's no point in ignoring those trembles, especially since a correct stance goes a long way to killing them. Believe me, I know all about the rough sea syndrome, although nowadays I take great pleasure in my ability to hold a six-power

His hair soaking on a rainy night, his coat sleeves and rifle smothered in mud and grass after a tumble down a steep bank, the author aims at a rabbit, confident that the rugged one-piece scope mount can handle such abuse.

scope frozen immobile on target for maybe two whole seconds. My job also helps here. As a sports photographer, I've found that an ability to hand-hold 300mm and 600mm lenses enables me to keep with the action. My rifle shooting has trained me to hold them steady – and vice versa. These long, very 'fast' lenses with massive front elements and costing thousands of pounds each, balance and weigh about the same as my rifle.

The final part of my scope's description is the most important to my mind. The 56mm refers to the diameter of its front lens. We photographers refer to the 'speed' of our lenses. If they're 'fast', that

means they let through a lot of light. I regard fast lenses as essential for keeping a bright image, and in close contact with the action.

A 56mm front lens in a scope is a rarity. That's why it's called a 'Moonlighter'. It's fast enough to allow me to shoot effectively in very low light levels – late dusk or even brilliant moonlight. My reason for buying it therefore becomes obvious. My fast scope allows me to be effective earlier and later in the day, it permits me to find quarry fast and aim quickly, and it transmits plenty of light when I'm out lamping rabbits. This means I don't need so bright a lamp that it spooks my quarry before I get within range.

Some scopes have slightly different optical systems, allowing them a wider angle of view. These wide-angle scopes, which often have a rectangular sight picture, help to sight on to quarry fast under tricky conditions.

You have to take care that the scope you choose will actually fit your rifle and mounts. A fast front lens is a big beast and, in my one-piece mount, my Moonlighter clears the air chamber by a fraction of an inch.

Keeping the Scope Clean

Another important point about my front lens is that it is recessed by about an inch. This keeps rain and drizzle off it. A deep recess is vital because of the rain splashes and wind turbulence around your body which can push water droplets in all directions. Even with this recess, though, you have to accept that most shooters face the wind when they're stalking. That's when the rain gets blown all over the glass, blurring the sight picture. You can make matters much easier for yourself if you take along a pad of kitchen paper to give the lens a periodic wipe.

The rear lens is awfully exposed to the weather. But you can buy a rubber eye-cup for most scopes. This recesses the lens well away from the wet. Linked, flip-up front and back covers are available, but they don't allow such quick shooting because they have to be flipped first. Nevertheless, this may not be an important consideration for your type of shooting.

A scope is a precision optical instrument, and the glass should be treated with care. Most lenses in scope sights are coated nowadays. You can see them flash different colours in different lights. Coatings improve the percentage of light which the

lenses transmit and reduce the amount they absorb or reflect away. They can be quite soft, as can some types of lens glass, so they might be ruined by insensitive cleaning.

Grit is the killer – it's in the fibres of your handkerchief and embedded in most dusters. The best lens cleaner is soft toilet paper. It doesn't scratch. However, before you wipe away any smears, take a soft artist's paintbrush and sweep all the dust from the lenses. With the grit gone, you can polish. Usually a wipe with the soft paper will be enough. Sometimes a huff of breath will be needed to remove a spot of dirt, but this can produce smears. Fibres from the paper are easy to sweep away with the brush. Keep it clean and dry, or it will create its own smears. Don't scrub at the glass, and be reluctant to clean too often. These suggestions apply to your sun and shooting glasses, too.

A scope needs to be waterproof or the lenses will steam up inside at every possible opportunity. The best scopes are filled with nitrogen gas and then sealed, eliminating this problem for ever. It is a point worth bearing in mind when a particularly cheap price tag catches your attention. However, one problem in life is that the most expensive usually works out being the cheapest, but only in the long run. A scope with built-in obsolescence isn't likely to do wonders for your shooting.

I don't claim that my Moonlighter is the best scope in the world. But I've had it for a long time and I've come to understand its idiosyncracies. It has yet to let me down and has shown itself capable of putting up with quite a lot of rough treatment without the point of zero shifting. There are better models around; I know, because my friends tote them. Maybe I'll change – one day.

Something that irritates me about my

The post and cross-hairs reticule targeted on a carrion crow.

scope is that the adjusting knob on top, which alters the elevation, has no cover. On many scopes, the two adjusting screws have screw-off caps. You remove these down on the zeroing range, twiddle the screws until you can knock a fly off a wall at thirty yards, then screw the caps back on to protect the settings. The windage adjustment on my scope conforms to this norm, but the elevation knob is free to catch the side of my coat as I'm walking along and tweak itself up or down a few notches. It does nothing for critical consistency and I'm afraid it'll eventually have to go.

The adjustment controls on most scopes move the point of impact one-quarter of an inch at 100 yards per click.

At 25 yards, four clicks will be required to adjust the zero by a quarter-inch.

Reticules

Underneath those knobs are what is called the reticule. This consists of cross-hairs, or whatever combination of broad lines, fine lines and circles you may find most suitable for hunting. Although most big makers offer a variety of reticules for each model, most hunters prefer just two – the dual-X cross-hairs and the post and cross-hair. Each is as good as the other, making personal preference the most important criterion.

The post and cross-hair is excellent for

taking moving targets. The single horizontal cross-hair makes a reliable guide for swinging along the same plane as your target, while the very obvious post is reminiscent of the old-style foresight. It's a good reticule for dim light conditions because of that very obvious central post.

Dual-X cross-hairs, which taper from broad lines to a super fine cross in the middle, can be hard to see in some conditions. This is particularly noticeable when shooting in thick, well-shaded foliage. Under these conditions it is often hard to find the quarry in the first place, especially with a high-magnification scope, and the

fine cross-hairs are hard to see in the poor light. Many reticules glow silver under these conditions, when light hits them through the eyepiece.

However, this design of reticule provides a very clear, precise and uncluttered sight picture under most conditions. It is also good for measuring how far off to aim for high wind and long range. This is because the fine cross-hair in the middle looks to be about a quarter-inch wide. It has become instinctive for me to think in terms of giving my quarry an extra quarter of a cross-hair for distance, and maybe just a fraction of another for windage. It

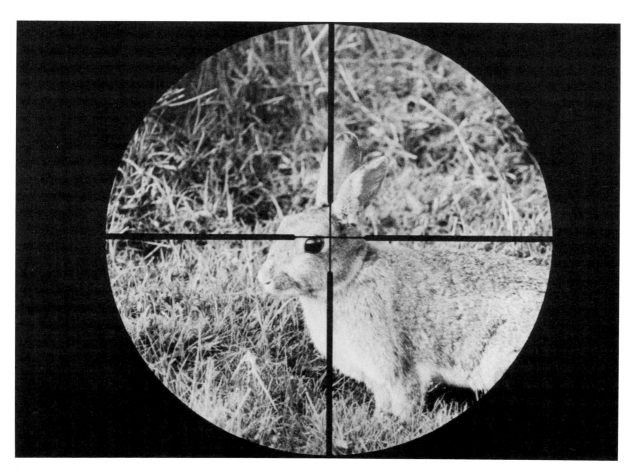

The dual-X reticule zeroed on a rabbit. Would that we could always hold it this still!

Richard Beaugie demonstrates the importance of looking straight through the middle of the scope.

all becomes intuitive after a while – and deadly accurate.

The reticule is quite unlike a rear open sight when you come to adjust it. The whole thing moves up and down, and side to side. Yet the lenses are arranged so that, despite these movements, the reticule always looks to be floating precisely in the middle of the lens. I suppose this is as good as saying that if it doesn't float, don't buy the scope. Floaters are pretty standard nowadays.

Moving closer to the eye, you see the magnification adjustment ring which, for me, stays fixed on six power. Although you can buy some lovely little low-power scopes, I think that a four- or six-power is about ideal for effective hunting, with the upper figure requiring a steadier hand

in use. Best to start low and work up, perhaps.

Behind this are the focus locking ring and the focus adjusting ring. The lens is fitted inside an eye piece which you can screw in or out to adjust the focus. You do this after selecting your magnification, if you have a sight of variable power. Once in focus – something I find hard to achieve because my eye keeps adjusting with the lens – you lock the setting with the knurled ring. A purely aesthetic consideration is that it is nice to keep the maker's insignia pointing upwards rather than away to one side.

For accurate shooting it is essential that both reticule and sight picture are in sharp focus together or else you'll have trouble with parallax. This is important because we shoot at the short ranges where parallax is most noticeable. If your scope is badly set up, the point of impact will appear to move in relation to the cross-hair according to how you look through the scope. Even with scopes that aren't corrected for parallax at close ranges, airgunners can forget about the problem provided that we always look through the centre of the optics and set the focus up correctly at the beginning.

It's no coincidence that the easily unscrewable focus adjustment should sport the importer's name. There aren't many scope manufacturers in the world, and several standard models have a habit of appearing in different liveries. Often the only change is the maker's name on the focusing ring.

Arresting Recoil

A characteristic of piston-operated air rifles which isn't widely appreciated is that they recoil quite fiercely. A .22 rimfire is a pussy-cat compared to a .22 air firearm. Even standard, moderate hunting rifles have quite a kick. It is strong enough in some rifles to shake the scope off zero – even damage the reticule. However, this is exceptional and normally a consequence of tinkering. There are firms that specialise in tuning in power while

Some critical bits, particularly the rugged one-piece scope mount with an arrestor block behind it. The vertical hold adjustment on the scope readily loses zero when caught on clothing or shrubbery while stalking. The inverted scope mount holds a lamp for night shooting. At this time only, the magnification of the sight is upped to nine power. Normally it is set at six power. At far right is the focusing ring to avoid parallax errors. Beneath it, the safety catch. Use it.

tuning out recoil.

Recoil can do two things. It'll cause the scope to creep backwards in the mount, and the mount to creep backwards in the rails. When mounting a scope make sure that everything is screwed down really tightly and that an arrestor block is keyed to the rifle to stop any chance of creeping.

It's simply a block of metal which keys into the scope rails (also known as the scope ramp) on top of the rifle and immediately behind the rear mount. On an HW 80, an Allen screw is keyed into one of the little holes between the rails which are designed for this purpose. Different rifles use other versions of this trick. Your dealer will help if you're uncertain. I don't think it's a question of shooting a rifle and finding out whether the scope mounts are solid enough. They may be then, but could slacken in time. A recoil arrestor makes doubly sure, and for the price it's worth the peace of mind. Besides, it takes some of the stress off the rails when the rifle recoils, preventing premature wear.

Mounting the Scope

The barrel of most scopes, between the fore and aft tapers, is practically of a standard diameter, permitting a wide range of mounts to be fitted for attachment to the rifle. For consistent shooting, there's only one type of mount to be fitted – a rock-solid one.

It is sensible to accept that no matter how much care you take of your rifle, it will get some pretty hard knocks from time to time. You'll feel very much more confident if your mount is so secure that it would take a bomb to shift the scope off zero. The only way to achieve this is with a rugged one-piece mount.

Several firms make these for most different designs of rail. This is because the scope ramp varies in width between different makes of rifle. Some come with recoil arrestor devices built in.

Then there are the widely-used two-piece mounts, one fitted forward, the other aft of the scope barrel. They're cheap, cheerful, and moderately sturdy in use. However, you can't expect mounts with such small areas of contact between scope and rifle to be rock-solid. The fact that they aren't connected rigidly together, as on a one-piece mount, allows them to flex under stress – bye-bye zero!

A compromise which allows you to use both open sights and a scope at the same time is the raised two-piece mount. It's like the previous variety, but instead of holding the scope as low on to the rifle as possible, it raises it high enough for you to see through the iron sights beneath it.

The idea is a dead loss. There is no logical reason for alternating between open and scope sights – unless the scope is of such inferior design that it shouldn't be there in the first place. The practical disadvantage is that the scope's line of sight is so high above the pellet's line of fire that it's extremely hard to estimate windage and elevation because of the greater angles involved. Obviously, a scope on stilts is the least solid of the lot.

A scope needs to be carefully mounted if it is to be effective. Start off by fixing the mount and recoil arrestor as far forward in the rails as possible. This will give you more room to slide the optics backwards and forwards while you make final adjustments.

An essential part of mounting a scope is to remember what is termed 'eye-relief'. This is the distance between the rear lens and your eye when it percieves the clearest sight picture – usually about three inches. Any closer will spoil the picture. Sometimes you'll see people hold their eye right up to the rear lens. This is quite wrong. Besides making it almost impossible to

How not to mount a scope sight. The sight can easily be twisted in these mounts, and even though the rifle has a recoil arrestor at the back of the ramp, the rear mount hasn't been placed tight up to it.

see the sight picture, there's a high risk of the gun's recoil banging the scope back into your eyebrow with sufficient force to require stitches. Even a mild clout will make your eyes water.

Shoulder the rifle in your standard way and slide the scope, making sure it doesn't topple on to the floor, through the mount until the sight picture is perfect. Now mark the place in pencil on the scope barrel. Place the rifle lengthways in a vice, on the back of a chair or whatever, pointing at the wall and keeping it quite upright. Now look through the front lens, with the rifle perfectly balanced, and you'll get a clear picture of the cross-hairs. Twist

the scope until the vertical hair is upright like the rifle. This way you'll know that any changes in the elevation won't make your shots start creeping off to one side. For this reason it is wise to get into the habit of mounting the rifle squarely in your shoulder.

This has particular relevance for some makes of rifle which have barrels that droop slightly in relation to the air chamber. Sometimes there isn't enough adjustment in the vertical hold to raise the point of impact high enough to compensate for the droop. This can be rectified by fitting a layer or two of card between the scope and the rear mount.

Eye-relief. It's important to fix the scope where it provides the best picture of the target.

Once everything is spot–on, put the tops of the mounts over the scope and tighten down the screws. Do a few turns on each screw at a time to prevent your careful arrangement from being distorted. Once everything is firmly battened down, make a final check for alignment before turning on the torque. Don't mutilate the screws with excessive force, but make sure they're firmly home.

All you need do then is to zero the rig. This is covered in the chapter on shooting straight.

4 Accessories and Clothing

All sorts of things add to the pleasure of a day afield with an air rifle. It may be a pair of boots – or a badge. In this chapter we'll be taking a look at some of the items which will ease and expand your enjoyment of the sport.

Silencers

It is one of life's neat little ironies that in America, where you can buy a machine-gun over the counter, silencers are illegal. In Britain, where some people would like catapults to be banned from sale, there are no restrictions against using a silencer.

It's a fairly simple piece of equipment, just a tube full of baffles to kill the crack from the muzzle. There are various ways of fixing one to the barrel of a rifle, so make sure that your dealer knows what rifle you want it to fit. Some makes require an adaptor to be fitted. It is possible to use different rifles fitted with their own peculiar adaptors and to screw on a silencer as and when it is required. My favourite is a permanent fixture that tapers neatly on to the barrel, being held in place by a discreet screw.

From the butt end, especially with a piston rifle, the metallic clang of firing is highly audible. However, that is because it is right up close to the ear. Stand fifty yards away and get somebody to fire towards you (no, not straight at you!), and you'll hear hardly a whisper from the rifle. The pellet hitting home makes a much louder crack.

It used to be thought that a silencer affected the performance of a rifle. This idea is generally discounted nowadays as being too slight to be significant.

Slings

Some people like a sling on their rifle – I don't. However a broad, leather strap that clips to a special fitting on the stock and the barrel not only looks good but makes a rifle more comfortable to carry for long periods. Leather-workers have always ensured that rifle slings remain works of art.

My decision to unscrew the fittings from my rifle is based on field experience. Both the sling and the fittings (even when the sling isn't clipped on) have the serious flaw of clattering or clicking at precisely the wrong moment. That moment is when you're shouldering the rifle for a well-deserved shot after a successful, long-range stalk.

The air rifle is most effective when used close to your quarry. Any sound this near is bound to attract intense scrutiny and it is infuriating to see a departing scut as your bunny legs it into the brambles.

The sling decides to draw attention to itself by catching on a button, or scraping as the rifle comes to shoulder. The shame is that after all that hard work, you didn't

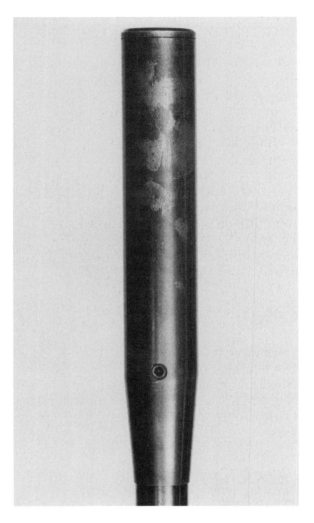

A silencer effectively reduces the sound of a shot. This one, with the author's fingerprints etched by battery acid, is held in place by a discreet screw.

The performance of entangling an arm in a sling before firing strikes me as a complicated distraction from the real issue.

Binoculars

A pair of binoculars is useful for spotting quarry to stalk and to work out how to get there. It also enables you to keep watch on your quarry, to find out how it is behaving – even how numerous it is – when planning a sortie. Tasco make a good pair of waterproof binoculars in a soft green colour and they are excellent value for money.

Knife

Most essential is a knife. Some people would have you tote a Swiss army knife that's crammed with gadgets. However, I don't anticipate that any screws will fall out of my rig, and if any horses have stones in their hoofs they'll have to hobble to the blacksmith in the village. I'm quite content with one sturdy blade.

You can use a sheath-knife or a clasp-knife. Just remember, when closing a clasp-knife, to press the back of the blade against the palm of your left hand while keeping the fingers of your right hand out of the way along the back and sides of the handle. That way you won't need any stitches. Ideally there should be a catch to lock the blade when it's in use.

A big knife is not necessary. Indeed, the extra metal requires the edge to be honed at a steep angle, preventing the blade from slipping in behind the cutting edge. A four-inch knife is perfectly adequate. The blade should be kept sharp on a steel or oilstone (not coarse carborundum, please) so that it can be used for adjusting the countryside while you're building hides and firing points. It'll cut quite thick

even get to see the rabbit in the sights. As I have yet to discover a sling which doesn't become an encumbrance at the moment of shooting, I never use one.

I see some shooters twisting the sling around their arm and wrist. This is completely unnecessary with any air rifle. The real purpose is to get a clear sight picture as soon as possible and squeeze off an accurate shot before your quarry moves.

branches if you work round them.

Naturally, the knife will be used for cleaning game for the table. Again the blade is useful for jointing legs and wings, but the point needs to be as sharp as a pin and bright like a scalpel for paunching rabbits and removing the breasts from pigeons. The steel in my knife isn't the best in the world so occasionally I use a fine file to restore the point and make good any little notches.

I've lost countless knives over the years, particularly lovingly-honed home-made favourites. On several occasions I've had to retrace my steps by a mile or more to find the knife sitting on a mossy bank, precisely where I remembered last putting it. This is an awareness that every hunter should develop because one becomes fond of a good knife and it may be expensive to replace.

Once I lost a knife and couldn't recall where I'd last used it. However, I'd had the misfortune to wound a rabbit which just made it to its hole. It was practically dead, but I could see it sitting well out of arm's reach down its burrow. Then it twitched a little further around a corner and out of sight. I continued my hunt, but in vain. Later, it occurred to me that maybe the knife had fallen out of my pocket while I was up-ended over the burrow. I walked a mile and a half through the windy, drizzly night until I found the row of bushes that marked the warren. There on the moist sandy soil lay my knife – and the rabbit. Occasionally – very occasionally – a hit rabbit which you think is dead in its burrow will struggle back out to die in the open. I've no idea why; but it's always worth pausing for.

It is quite easy to build up a sixth sense about your knife. I keep my clasp-knife in one specific pocket of my shooting coat. Its presence is now familiar to me and the lack of that weight and small lump near my stomach instantly tell me if I've forgotten

to put it back there. I also have an automatic habit of checking it's there before I move off again.

You can also build an awareness of a sheath-knife on a belt, although I no longer use one. It means there's something rigid attached to me while I'm stalking along, and I find this intrusive. I wouldn't advise anybody to carry a sheath-knife in their pocket – even in a stout sheath. If you slip over and land on the knife you may end up with a badly gashed leg, as happened to a friend of mine. When a similar accident befell me, the blade snapped free from the handle before it could penetrate deeply. I was lucky.

A pair of gardener's secateurs are a more practical alternative to a knife for cutting branches when making hides. They're useful for all sorts of trimming operations, like when you have to open up a stalking alley through heavy cover. This is often the only practical way to get close to some warrens and woodpigeon roosts. A quick trim each year keeps them open.

Lamps

Night shooting requires special equipment, particularly a lamp. I prefer to use one that's mounted on my forehead. I designed and built my own from a General Electric GE 4547 4.25 volt sealed beam which is mounted in a block of polyethylene foam. A broad band of elastic keeps it on my forehead, and the lead passes over my crown to provide extra support. This is held at the right length by knots each side of the length of elastic. The two ends of this are stitched together at the back of my head, trapping the wire between them. The whole unit, except the back, is wrapped with black tape to prevent leakages of light shining on to my

A scope-mounted lamp for rabbit shooting at night. The battery is strapped to a piece of rope which serves as a belt to be worn around the waist.

face. For a similar reason I fitted a small hood to prevent light spilling all around me. This hood is made from a child's seaside bucket and is also covered with black tape.

The lead has an on/off switch fitted at breast pocket height and ends in two clips. These fit the six-volt motorbike battery which I wear around my waist. It is taped to a length of rope which serves as a belt. That way any acid spills don't wreck a good belt – nor rot the pockets of my shooting coat. It is best if you can get a sealed battery.

You don't want too bright a light for rabbiting at night or, once they realise that lamps are a threat, your quarry will hightail to its burrow before you're in range. A good beam from your forehead will reflect back into the scope much more brightly than one being carried by a mate. The positioning on the forehead is important.

I walk around with it in the middle of my head, looking to catch little orange gleams in the grass as the lamp bounces back from the red blood cells at the back of a rabbit's eyes. This is the reason why so many flash photographs produce subjects with red eyes – the planes of flash and lens are too close together. The effect is eliminated by moving one further away from the other. Do this with your lamp and you won't see those tell-tale orange gleams.

The problem with a lamp on your

forehead is that as soon as you mount the rifle, the beam points away to your right. You solve this by slipping it over the left eye before bringing the rifle on to aim. It doesn't take much practice to get the hang of it.

Of course it's quite possible to go lamping with a friend who carries a powerful torch. But you'll have to stand close together if much light is to bounce back into the scope. Under some circumstances it is best to shine the torch over the shooter's shoulder – or under his arm if the grass isn't too long.

A totally useless abomination is the torch which is designed to be clamped to the rifle or, at its tasteless extreme, to be screwed on to the front end. Such torches

naturally have their own batteries. Even so, they aren't bright enough and the extra weight is more than enough to spoil your shooting. They also solve very little because you either need a separate lamp to scan the landscape for orange gleams, or you'll have to swing the rifle around all night. However, I have recently built one to clamp into a scope mount fitted upside-down on the scope of my rifle. My partner uses this when we shoot together, with a lead going to a belt-mounted battery. But even this changes the rifle's shooting characteristics slightly. It makes it shoot an inch and a half low. You can buy headlamps from several fishing tackle shops. But these are puny, too, being designed to allow sea anglers to re-bait

All the kit for a night's shooting – rifle, ammo, headlamp, rucksack, knife, dog-collar and slip lead.

hooks on the benighted beach without ramming the point into a thumb.

Rucksack

Another aid when shooting at night is a rucksack. Make sure it is made of cotton canvas, not nylon or any other material that rustles. Neither should it have buckles that tinkle, nor loose straps that flap and warn of your approach. It should have a good frame across the back and padded straps to support the weight of your catch. A belt across your waist will also allow heavy loads to be carried more lightly. Just make sure that you don't go over the top and buy too big a bag.

If you can fit twenty paunched rabbits into it, you'll have a good 50lb to carry home on your back. If you're like me and hunt wild places, you won't be able to use any other form of transport than your back. After two miles over rugged country, I'm always very glad when I can unburden my load into the boot of the car. A rucksack of excessive size is also a liability in a high wind, acting like a sail to catch every buffet and throw you off aim.

You will also find that your accuracy deteriorates as the bag fills. This is because the weight of your bag causes the straps to pull more and more tightly into your shoulders. It becomes harder and harder for you to mount the rifle in that regular manner which produces all those consistent kills. You can avoid this either by taking along a partner to carry the bag or you can unload frequently, leaving bunnies in fox-proof stashes to be collected later.

You need to be quite fit for this sort of shooting, but even the fittest can severely damage their backs if a sack of bunnies is lifted incorrectly. I once bent down, picked up a bag holding half a dozen bunnies, and in the same movement swung it over my shoulder. After months of agony, my wrenched sacro-iliac joint ('twixt spine and pelvis) started to heal. Even so I would sometimes get sudden, severe cramps in both legs simultaneously when riding my motorbike – quite unnerving. Nearly ten years later it gives only the occasional twinge. Keep your back straight, and bend your legs. Tense both back and stomach muscles after catching hold of the sack, then straighten your legs, pushing your bottom in to prevent the weight making you stoop. This should prevent you from becoming immobilised on the moors at night with a slipped disc.

Clothing

Clothing is important, no matter what type of hunting you're into. I generally wear a pair of trousers and a coat that are part of the Kammo range by Sporting Developments Ltd. They are made from soft cotton canvas that has been printed with the Nato pattern of camouflage. This material doesn't rustle and enables me to stalk silently in even the quietest, stillest conditions. This is an obvious but important point. However, the Kammo coat is designed to let you sit down in damp corners and is fitted with a waterproof lining around the bottom. The trouble is that this rustles very slightly against the back of my legs, which is irritating. This feature is omitted from current styles.

Although this coat only lets through the heaviest downpours, I don't think you can beat genuine Nato-issue clothing. It is designed for battle conditions after all, and a waterproof sandwich inside the coat effectively seals out rain. Other points to watch for when buying camouflage are the zips and poppers. Zip tabs have a habit of tapping against the closed rows of zip teeth while you're walking along. You can silence these with a leather thong. Poppers are fitted rather like rivets to storm flaps. They have an annoying tendency to rattle.

The way to test the noise made by your clothing is to walk up and down your living room when the rest of the world has gone to bed and the house is silent. You'll then be able to hear all the tinkles, taps and rustles from your clothing – maybe also from the laces of your trainers and baggy trousers scraping together while you walk. They may sound insignificant to you, but I believe that rabbits in particular are adept at hearing sounds very high up the frequency range.

Creaky clothing makes its presence known to the rabbits well before you arrive, especially when you're out lamping on a quiet night. Their sensitive ears will pick up every sound you make. It's as though you're throwing out a bow wave of disturbance, like an ocean-going liner. That's why breeze in the grass is so useful to a stalker.

In summer it's often too warm to be encumbered by a coat, but you can buy camouflage shirts. If there isn't a suitable pellet pocket, take a snip of material from the tail and sew one on.

If you get too hot, you'll be plagued by flies trying to sup all those salty nutrients in your perspiration. A cap decreases the available dining area. Clean hair and face make you less attractive to them. If you're plagued by midges, get a repellent cream and smear it all over your face, neck, hands, wrists and ankles – all those points where midges can crawl in and start excruciatingly irritating itches. They can get through open-weave clothing without any problem at all.

There are some very strange camouflage outfits on sale, especially in markets and army surplus stores. You have to consider the background you will be seen against before choosing your outfit. Some

are so light and sandy in overall colour that they would be a perfect match for the rocks, boulders and dunes of the Libyan desert, but are totally inappropriate to northern woodland. That is why the Nato pattern scores so well.

Get a separate coat and trousers, not a one-piece Action Man suit. Besides looking ridiculous, they're made from a quilted, sandy-coloured camouflage material which has absolutely no resistance to wind or rain. No doubt this design will eventually be superseded by something a little more effective for our climate. Even so, one-piece suits really do restrict movements and, because of this, some of the contortions you get into while stalking cause the suit to rip open along the arm seams. Mine did.

But there is an even more important reason. One-piece suits have a very solid outline which is hard to conceal in such a raggedy place as woodland. You have only to look at the masters of woodcraft, the American pioneers and the Red Indians, to see how they felt on the subject. Their clothing was designed with ragged edges along the arms and legs, with thongs to break its outline. Camouflage itself goes a long way to achieve this, but the effect is enhanced by ample shoulders, pouch pockets, and the change of contour from coat bottom to trousers. For this reason I'm not too bothered that the pouch pockets on my Kammo coat have become bottomless, flapping bits of cloth thanks to battery acid. Before this destruction forced me to lash the battery to a rope around my waist, I used to keep my rabbiting battery in my pocket. They're now useless, so I've got nowhere to slip game, necessitating string to carry it hanging from my shoulder.

A big poacher's pocket is good for carrying game; or for more even balance when laden, having one on each side of the coat is better. Do yourself a favour and cover them with a wide flap made from a silky smooth material so that refugee fleas are deflected back to earth and can't crawl inside the waistband of your trousers.

I'd like to think that it was the pioneering spirit which made me take a knife to my trouser bottoms and cut them to length. They arrived unfinished at the bottom and were so long, even for a long-legged chap like me, that they kept smothering my heels. Now the ends are slightly frayed, providing a broken line between leg and shoe. They're wearing well, too. I knew they would. What really happened was that I tripped up for the umpteenth time because of their flapping about; and I decided there and then that enough was enough, and sat down with my knife to hack them into shape.

Footwear

Another hint you can take from the Red Indian is the suppleness of his footwear. Many a wary white man lost his scalp through failing to detect the soft footfall of a supple moccasin. You'll never be able to stalk like a wraith in wellies or any other type of boot. These only have any use in thick mud or deep snow – times when your footfalls would squelch or creak in any footwear.

No matter what the weather or time of year, I usually wear a well-used pair of lace-up trainers. Don't tie the laces too tight or you'll restrict the blood circulation down there and make your feet ache or get cold when they shouldn't. It's easily done, because their glove-like characteristic doesn't leave much space for movement or the natural swelling that happens after you've walked a few miles. Don't buy a shoe if the heel has a hollow echo when it hits hard ground.

Trainers are thermally much more efficient than moccasins, but you'll need warm socks and good circulation to keep your feet comfortable. The thin soles enable you to feel the ground beneath your feet. When I'm stalking those final, silent yards, I take short steps, putting the heel down first, keeping my toes quite high. The heel goes down gently, feeling for the hardness of twigs, the springiness of leaves, or the yielding softness of earth or grass. Then I unroll my foot on to the ground, transferring the weight from the back, to the front of the heel, and on to the ball of the foot before taking the next step.

All the time, my feet are feeling the changing surface beneath them so that I have only to glance down occasionally to map my route. The ground is being tested during each step before my full body weight is committed to it. You can't do that in stiff soles or floppy old wellies. And when you get home, generally with wet, but warm, feet, a change of socks and footwear ensures you don't catch a chill. I can't remember the last time I caught one.

In the winter, however, you'll need more appropriate footwear. If you don't have to walk far, wear 'moon boots'. They really are the best thing going for keeping feet comfortably toasty while you're sitting in a hide. Most shooting and fishing shops stock appropriate models during the winter months. You must keep the insides dry though, else they won't be so efficient and you'll catch fungal infections between your toes. Damp conducts warmth, which is why non-absorbent fibres close to the skin force perspiration to pass right through. It can't soak in.

Very often you'll find good hunting in appalling weather conditions. I must confess that I love being out on the hills at night with a lamp, rifle and lurcher. My shooting partner and I have great times, but we've learned to dress for the weather. You get out on to the high tops when an east wind in February comes whistling straight from Siberia, and you soon come to a very obvious conclusion. It's cold.

Winter Wear

Keeping warm requires three considerations to be fulfilled. First, the clothing must trap layers of warm air close to your body, providing thermal efficiency by retaining a high degree of body heat. Second, it must be loose enough (but not too loose) to allow this warm air to exist, and permit movement and the free circulation of blood. Vests with tight armpits and slinky trousers will give you cold hands and feet. Third, this thermal layer must be sheltered from the wind by a layer of draught–excluding material – like a combat jacket.

In Siberian weather I wear a Damart vest, a nylon–fur one-piece body warmer (they're made for workers in freezer plants), and a sweater. I also have a nylon-fur waistcoat for when the temperature really plummets or I have decided to stake out some place in a hide all day and it's so cold that the frost doesn't respond to the sun. Over the top of all this goes my coat and camouflage trousers held up with a belt.

A cap is a good way to lag the loft; although when I'm out lamping on the hills, the exercise leaves me feeling glad if the heat can escape through my head. Thermal socks and gloves retain heat around those vulnerable areas where the blood supply is closest to the cold – the ankles and wrists.

On the hands I wear a pair of fingerless mitts. Millarmitts and other thermal mitts are good not just for keeping the hands warm, but also for smothering the pink blob which tells wary critters where a

hunter is lurking. This is where the peaked cap scores too, by shading the face.

The point is not made lightly because it is fundamental to all your camouflage. The coat and trousers may break up your outline, but unless you conceal all three of those pink blobs you'll spook game time after time, whether you're stalking or ambushing. I often wear light fingerless gloves and a cap, in summer and winter, for this purpose. Having grown a beard, I find that it complements my high collar and the cap in concealing my neck and face, allowing surreptitious glances beneath the peak to check the final deployment of my quarry.

I've tried face nets, but they really are uncomfortable and restrict my field of vision even if I enlarge the eye holes. They have the annoying habit of becoming permanently knotted into place, which is more than a little claustrophobic. Camouflage face paint is pretty abominable stuff. Dabs of dark brown will break up the outline, but they have to be big and dark enough to conceal as much pink as possible. It's unpleasant to remove, though, requiring cold cream or baby-wipes, and it smears on to the stock of your rifle and all bits of clothing that come within reach.

In snow, white clothing might seem to offer good camouflage. But you won't find much to hunt out in the unbroken wastes of snow. Most of your quarry will be in the woods where unbroken white will make you stand out from the dark background.

It is important to keep warm in winter, so that may mean taking along a tile of polyethylene foam to sit on in your hide, insulating your backside from the frost. This plastic foam is soft and flexible like polythene and its cells don't collapse when you sit on it. A waterproof cushion or a part-inflated air cushion will also do the job.

White clothing isn't essential for stalking in winter woodland because the snow cover is well broken.

To be cold while hunting means that your movements will be slow, unreliable, and stiff. It won't be long before you're fidgeting to get warm and comfortable, thinking of the logs crackling in the hearth at home. When the woodpigeons fly in to roost, you'll be gone. Maybe you'll turn round from the top of the hill as the sun dips over the horizon, intensifying the cold. You'll see the birds wheeling around, gliding into the trees around your hide. Perhaps your ears will catch the distant clatter of their wings.

My final piece of advice about clothing may not go down too well with your friends. In recent years, there has been an enormous increase in public awareness of hygiene. The soap powder manufacturers have joined in moral blackmail by telling everyone how clean everything they wear has to look, feel, and smell – else they're just slobs. This brainwashing is liable to make you fling your grubby camouflage garments in to the wash. Then they'll reek

50

of the latest shade of scented detergents, and the bunnies will be delighted at your willingness to let them scent you.

Think of your coat as an outer shell that needs to be brought indoors, no matter what objections, because a coat from a damp shed is about as comfortable as wet socks. This dryness will hinder the bacteria from multiplying, decreasing the smell. Don't wash a coat until you have to because the streaks of mud and rabbit, the coatings of rain and weather, and the aroma of leaf-mould, all help to disguise the scent of the man inside.

5 Shooting Straight

The ability to shoot straight is the bottom line, the final pay-off after buying and setting up the rifle and sight, finding somewhere to shoot, getting close to your quarry, then ultimately seeing its sight picture through the scope.

What happens next depends entirely on you. It's not simply a question of a hit or a miss because that is too flippant an attitude for the serious hunter. In most shooting sports there's a horrible grey area called wounding. It's your paramount duty to avoid this, at all costs.

It's always much more pleasing to watch your quarry slump, inert and unaware, the moment you squeeze the trigger. There's no reason why this shouldn't happen right from your first hunting expedition provided you remember one thing: when hunting live things, shoot well within the limits of your skill.

If you can't shoot a large coin off a fence post at twenty-five yards with five shots out of five, how can you expect a bunny to go down when your inexperience and buck fever are making you breathe loudly like a whale and your heart is hammering with excitement. Live quarry is not for practice. That's what plinking is for.

Stance and Grip

Learning to shoot true starts the first day you fire a rifle. Where it hits depends a great deal on how you hold it. This is because, each time you shoot, the body has to steady the rifle and absorb the recoil. Obviously, if you hold the rifle in the same way for each shot, the pellet arrives in the same place every time – give or take a wobble or two in inexperienced hands.

I hold my gun in my right shoulder, with the right elbow raised to create a solid pocket into which to tuck the butt. Fortunately the butt on my rifle is set some way below the line of air chamber and barrel so I don't have to droop my head to the side to see through the scope. This is a common fault and it isn't always caused by the rifle not fitting the shooter. But some guns do have very short stocks, especially at the toy end of the market. It is impossible for an adult to shoulder such a gun, even with only the heel of the butt in his shoulder, and his head twisted over the stock searching for a sight picture.

It's always much easier to shoot with a rifle that fits than to adapt to one that doesn't. Many off-the-peg rifles fit nowadays, and some that don't feel right to me may feel good to you. This is always important because you'll only hit things consistently if you feel comfortable with your rifle.

The point has to be emphasised because I've watched people go into contortions while trying to get the hang of something they have read in a book. After all, this is your hobby and it should feel good. Advice gets its authority from the giver but has to be interpreted by the recipient before it gains any practical value second-hand.

To my mind, the ability to shoot standing is essential, even though it is tricky to

The standing stance requires no more than a firm hold and easy balance. Once mastered, it can be adapted to different situations.

53

learn. Some suggestions on how to hold the rifle may help with this. With the butt firmly tucked into the shoulder, you should be able to squeeze the cheek-piece of the stock with your face and jawbone, with the sight picture clearly visible to the right eye. The right hand, clasped around the pistol grip, gently pulls the rifle into the shoulder. The left hand, supporting the front of the fore end, also adds a soft, firm pull that locks the rifle between its various points of contact with your body.

These points of contact, and the firm grip, do wonders for curing the dreaded trembles. But there is a more serious reason. When a powerful piston-operated rifle is fired, the recoil sets shock waves rushing up the barrel and down the stock. These have to go somewhere, but as they're already in motion before the pellet has left the barrel, they must be damped down in a precise, controlled way that doesn't alter from shot to shot.

The firm, soft grip helps, but stance is important too. Hold the rifle across your body with your weight on your left foot, the right foot keeping your balance. Just stand comfortably, hold the rifle steadily on target, and softly squeeze off the shot. You'll be amazed, when you're in the thick of the action, how easily you can forget to stand correctly. But unless your feet are properly planted, your balance won't be right, and neither will anything else until you're accustomed to firing from any position.

Follow-Through

Obviously it is what happens while you fire that matters. You should try to make squeezing the trigger an instinctive response to a perfect sight picture. There's that old woodie on the weathered branch of a dead, ivy-smothered tree. You centre the cross-hairs over its heart, and suddenly it is tumbling through the leaves without you being aware of a signal having passed between different sections of your brain.

This doesn't happen to begin with, of course, but it comes quite quickly if you practise frequently. Just concentrate on holding firmly on target, and the trigger release will be instinctive. The worst thing you can do is to think of squeezing the trigger as the final part of the sequence. The finish in rifle shooting and all sports skills, is the follow-through. Without it a kick won't find goal, a punch won't land, and a fly won't entice a trout.

In those skills, however, the follow-through allows a powerful movement to come to a halt. In shooting, the effort centres around killing trembles and getting the sight picture steady. The follow-through ensures that you don't tweak the trigger sharply nor alter the rifle's position while the pellet is still travelling up the barrel. There should be no change in the position of the cross-hairs as the pellet zips home. This way you can see where it hits and you'll have perfect control over the recoil. This is why a subtle trigger mechanism is so essential.

You can see through the sight whether you're jogging the trigger, instead of squeezing it as softly as though there's a thistle spine sticking into the pad of your finger. Just shoulder the rifle, unloaded, centre on a mark, and squeeze the trigger. Do it a few times and it soon becomes obvious how easy it is for that tiny movement to destroy a perfectly-aligned sight picture. It's the commonest cause of missing.

Triggers are squeezed by the pad on the tip of the finger. They're not meant to slot into the joint below that pad. That squeeze is the final commitment, and it should happen with a resolute delicacy and the confidence that your cross-hairs will stay on mark for at least the next half-second.

The minimum requirement is a positive mental attitude to it all. Never tweak and hope. Flukes don't count – they wound.

You have to remember that you and your rifle are a live combination and that it'll take a crate or two of ammo and many hours – some enjoyable and some frustrating – to get to know each other well. To start with, you can only develop good habits and take it from there. Ultimately the accretion of experience pays off and instead of worrying about mastering the techniques, you're using them to express yourself by confidently killing in difficult situations.

For this reason alone I advise everybody to buy the best combination they can afford – and preferably the one they've set their heart on – and use only that one for practically all their shooting. A consistently high killing edge doesn't develop if a shooter keeps chopping and changing between outfits.

In the meantime a steady stance, a careful squeeze, and a considered follow-through will bang plenty of shots into the bull's-eye. You'll also find that the stance I recommend keeps your arms well away from your chest, allowing you to breathe freely. So it is up to you how you slot the trigger pull into your breathing rhythm. One way is to take a shallow breath, hold it, squeeze softly, and breathe out. It's always good to get into regular habits, though, and I think that most shooters pause their breathing for a few seconds while they concentrate on the final instant of loosing off a shot.

Achieving Consistency

Regular habits result in consistent performance, and this is important when shooting air rifles. So much depends on how the shock of the recoil is transferred to the body. This will always be the same if you hold and fire the rifle the same way each time. Problems come when you alter one of the variables by more than a small amount.

I know that if I shoot prone, with my elbows resting on the ground, my shot will flip an inch to the left. But for total inaccuracy, I have only to support the barrel on a branch for the pellets to flip three inches high and scatter to left and right. I didn't realise this many years ago when I built a hide overlooking a glade in a small copse. The place was teeming with rabbits, pigeons and game, and my hide would have withstood a Viking onslaught. Big boughs were smothered with gorse. I could sit on my log and pop the barrel through many a gap. By resting it on a branch I was able to centre the crosshairs unmovingly on my quarry, then squeeze. It was dreadfully discomfiting to see absolutely no sign of my pellet for shot after shot. I didn't realise that the recoil was causing the barrel to bounce off the boughs.

Provided you remember that you and your rifle are a living combination, you'll have no problem learning to shoot from different positions. Frequently you'll be able to steady your arm, but that's not the same as resting it. Remember that much has to do with the balance of your weight, so it is best if you can shoot without having to depend on walls and trees to rest on. Likewise it is a fallacy to lean your shoulder against anything while firing. The recoil will instantly twist you off target and flip the pellet to one side.

Muzzle flip is part of a rifle's recoil pattern. In serious cases you can fit a special weight to the end of the barrel – sometimes made in the form of a sleeve covering the entire length – in order to damp it down. To my mind this smacks of clumsiness and poor design. A well-built rifle shouldn't be jumpy. However, powerful hunting weapons develop special

Shooting in the prone position – note the angle between the rifle and the shooter's body.

stresses, but I'm not worried that my muzzle will flip when I shoot prone. The factor doesn't intrude because I don't let it. I compensate by aiming an inch to the right and half an inch low. It is always a good idea, where possible, to have a few warm-up shots. If your grouping seems to have decided to decamp to a different part of the target, bring it back into line by aiming off.

The standing stance gives you the independence and versatility to take any shot as it presents itself. You can hold the same basic position even when you sit, kneel or crouch. There are few circumstances under which this free-style type of stance will be found wanting. The hunter's problem is that opportunities happen at odd times. You'll be half over a fence and a rabbit will suddenly stand upright in the grass not thirty yards away. Or you'll be crouching under an overhanging branch while stalking a distant pigeon, and another – if not the same one – will swoop into the tree next to you. What a gift. Don't fluff it.

It helps, in the early days, to see yourself in a mirror with the rifle mounted at your shoulder. This is the best way to find out whether you lean the rifle in towards your cheek rather than hold it upright. This small point can prove to be important.

The problem is generally most evident with rifles of large calibre, and where the target is far off. If you tilt a rifle, elevation and windage adjustments on the sight will never be as accurate as they should be. Because most shooting is over short ranges, this error isn't noticeable. Nevertheless, be upright, and of good habits. These factors are all determined by the way in which an air rifle performs. The pellet is given a slight vertical boost to overcome gravity – it rises to intersect the line of sight. After a few yards of flight above this line, the pellet intersects it

again at the point of zero. This is the distance which gives you the best combination of sight line and pellet trajectory.

Zeroing Rifle and Scope

You can calibrate your own rifle on a day when the air is still and not too hot or cold. Make a target from a sheet of card, with the bull marked as a cross with a long vertical line, like the shape of a sword, hilt uppermost.

Start at five yards and aim for the centre of the cross every time. With a batch of five shots each time, the groups will start low, rising to the point of zero at about ten yards, above it at fifteen yards, and falling back to zero at twenty-five yards. By this time the cross in the target will be a mess, but the cross-hairs of your scope will align with what is left to show where the middle was.

The following groups are the interesting ones, especially out past sixty yards, with the five-yard increments showing as huge gaps between the successive groups as they drop down the blade of the imaginary sword. You can test how the breeze affects performance by firing at a similar target, set on its side. You really need to do this standing up because there's not much wind close to the ground, except in a wide open field. Not much happens your side of twenty-five yards, but past that the pellet is losing its zip quite rapidly. It is starting to destabilise, and a strong wind will whip it away for ever. There is only one purpose to any of these experiments – a greater awareness of how your rig performs under varying conditions.

The lighter the pellet, the flatter and faster the trajectory. Thus the point of zero is less important in .177 than it is when you're lobbing .22 pellets. However, you'll find in practice that twenty-five

It's tempting to rest the rifle on a solid branch, but direct contact exaggerates muzzle flip. Always rest on something soft, like your hand.

yards is a handy range at which to zero the elevation (vertical hold). The point of impact will only be a fraction lower at thirty yards and so barely worth considering. The pellet could have dropped an inch at forty yards, and three inches at fifty yards. This is only significant if you forget to compensate. No law states that the cross-hairs have to coincide with the point of impact at all times.

This consideration is fundamental to all good shooting. I prefer to be completely confident that my cross-hairs match the rifle's point of impact, and adjust my point of aim to cope with changing wind and range. If I start fiddling around with the setting I become totally confused, because I have yet to find a scope sight whose dials of numbers, notches and little white lines bear any relation to the changing point of impact. I know that field target shooters are dab hands at doing these fiddly calculations between shots, but I try to let inspiration rather than science rule my life. I know almost unconsciously that half an inch high and a little off to the left is just the spot to aim at to send that crow tumbling from its tree-top.

The important thing, yet again, is consistency. By always zeroing at one specific range, like twenty-five yards for .22 or thirty for .177, it eventually becomes second nature to assess how far off to aim to compensate for a side wind and how high to hold for long range.

For maximum precision, it is easiest to zero the windage (horizontal hold) at a much greater range than that when setting elevation, because any inaccuracy becomes more apparent. I'm talking here of only an extra fifteen to twenty yards because if you try to push the trick too far you'll get duff readings through pellets becoming unstable in flight at extreme range.

Even after many years of shooting, I frequently have to think twice about which way to twiddle the sight adjustments if they have been knocked off zero. The simple rule is that if you wish to move the point of impact to the left, move the rear sight or scope reticule to the left. The same applies to vertical hold, too. But never be in too much of a hurry to start fiddling. Shoot a couple of groups and ask yourself not only how good the groups are, but if they show any significant change in the point of impact.

It could be that a scattering around the bull has nothing to do with the sights but with how you are feeling. Maybe there was an undetected change in stance, or a mechanical fault on the rifle – like a slack barrel hinge. You'll save hours of frustration if you steer well clear of tinkering with the sights when you know in your heart of hearts that you're not shooting well that day. You'll also save on frustration when zeroing if you have a dozen or so warm-up shots to chase out the cobwebs before you get started.

Elevation Compensation

When calculating where to aim, the general rules need to be modified under certain circumstances. The one that I encounter most often is the rabbit that moves closer and closer towards me while I'm out lamping at night. When it is about three yards away and a total blur in the scope, it will stop, sit up, and stare at me. Under these circumstances my line of sight is high above that of the pellet, so I have to aim an inch high, or sometimes more. The fact that the bunny is blurred makes it hard to find a mark to aim at.

Even worse, try hitting a pigeon which lands in a tree immediately above your head. Aim straight at it, with the cross-hairs stark on that mauve breast, squeeze off, and the bird will clatter away without shedding a feather. Gravity is pulling on the pellet from behind this time. But the rifle's sighting system has been set to compensate for gravity pulling from beneath the trajectory. Now the pellet is not pulled back down to the line of sight by gravity, instead, it flies off behind you, missing wide. You compensate by aiming well low.

When you fire up a hill, or into a tall tree from afar, gravity exerts a stronger pull on a pellet than over the flat, so you will sometimes feel the need to give an extra inch if the range is a bit distant. Yet the problem is reversed when you're shooting downhill. The pellet doesn't slow and drop beneath the line of sight as quickly as you'd expect, causing you to miss over the top. So if you're shooting downwards, give it an inch less, or thereabouts. All I can do is make you aware of these problems. It's up to you to try 'em and see. Place rows of conkers, knobs of chalk, or whatever at different ranges at the bottom of a steep hill, but within your normal range, and find out how much you have to aim off target with your outfit.

Effective Range

For practical purposes, the effective ranges of .22 and .177 are about the same. But, to my mind, one of the greatest challenges of an air rifle is that it forces you to study woodcraft and get within telling range of your quarry. The further away you are from your mark, the more accurate and experienced you need be to hit it. The risk of wounding is greater, especially since the pellet is losing energy as it cuts through the wind and weather. So it may not hit with enough force to do lethal damage – be your aim impeccable.

The whole art of hunting with an air rifle is to be sure that when you slip the

trigger, your little missile goes precisely where you intend and produces the required effect. No matter how much whizz you tune into your rifle, it is always better to creep a little bit closer and turn confidence into certainty. If in doubt, stay your hand. There will always be plenty of more certain opportunities. Inaction, with a natural tinge of frustration if your quarry spots you too soon, is always preferable to the after-taste of guilt when wounded game isn't retrieved to the bag.

In a book like this, which covers all types of rifle from off-the-shelf junior airguns through to customised firearms, it is impossible to lay down hard and fast yardages as to how far you should stretch ranges. Out in the woods and fields, opportunities present themselves in different ways and you need sound woodcraft if a bird in the bush is to become a bird in the hand. Much also depends on the nature of your mark. If a big buck rabbit appears at fifty yards, it could be a great shot with the right outfit. But a tough target like that requires quite some clout, preferably to the head, to stop it in its tracks. Even with an FAC weapon I'd prefer to be within thirty yards, just to make sure, despite the fact that when I'm on form the longer range wouldn't defeat me. Now if that were a mouse clambering around in a bramble bush, a hit anywhere would be fatal. If you're feeling anti-mouse, and it's not a rare one, this would make a perfectly respectable mark.

Attitude and Fitness

A great deal of accuracy comes from how you're feeling. I remember having a great time in my garden one day, scoring group after group well within an inch at twenty yards while standing in my free-style position. Then the doorbell went. It was

The author pretending to be macho.

a friend whom I hadn't seen in years. After the rejoicing I went out to fetch the rifle but we stayed for a few shots. My groups were wild, as I was much too excited.

You have to feel good to shoot well, and very good to shoot brilliantly. Tiredness blunts the killing edge as surely as overstretched emotions. Physical fitness is essential, especially to the stalker. Creeping over the ground means that you're sometimes standing, sometimes crouching, sometimes crawling with only elbows and toes touching the earth. If you can't hold your rifle without it teetering in your grasp, a few press-ups each day will do wonders to your arms and shoulders – the main weight bearers.

Ideally a stalker should be able to walk a steep hill and still take a killing shot even with a marked increase in breathing and pulse rate. Severe cases of wheezing and shakes should be taken as sharp reminders that hunting is a more healthy waste of time than others. If you can't hold a steady bead after a long hike, then take a rest about fifty yards before reaching your firing position. This way you avoid the quarry getting wind of you while your breathing returns to normal. Such a practice is much more intelligent than blurting up on your quarry and missing.

Woodland stalking is the closest I know to yoga. Not only is a soft, sensitive footstep essential, but sometimes you have to insinuate yourself between branches, like a snake, without letting them scrape your clothing. All this requires co-ordinated control of every muscle in your body. A full session out in the woods can leave you feeling shattered the next day, especially if you aren't used to it. Your body, after all, is a stand on which you are resting a precision instrument. If the stand isn't up to keeping the rifle on target when opportunity smiles, how can you taste the sweetness of success?

Practice and Targets

Practice is the only way to get good at anything. Will yourself to shoot straight and take care of each shot. Precision will only come if you reach out for it. This doesn't mean that you need to spend hours down at the range in the freezing cold. One of England's Olympic gold medallist shooters once told me that he practises in front of the television. After all, your main problem lies in training your muscles not to wobble while you're holding the rifle on aim, then squeezing off without it moving. The rifle doesn't need to be loaded or cocked for this, indeed it shouldn't be unless you really don't like chat-show hosts all that much. This sort of regular handling does great things for consistent shooting afield.

It is outdoors, though, in the spinneys and copses that you can have all the practice you like, especially with airgun ammunition being so delightfully cheap. Fungi, crab-apples, dead twigs, leaves – all sorts make great impromptu targets that teach you to come on aim, hold and squeeze in one fluent, unhurried but precise movement. Nothing is gained by wobbling about on target. If this happens, it means that your muscles aren't yet strong enough to handle the weight of your outfit.

In the garden, you can practise by plinking at all sorts of things from tin cans to bottle tops. Each shot provides greater experience, and in this sport most of us will be only as good as the number of careful shots we have fired, and the misses we have mulled over in our minds.

Practice makes perfect, but how and where you do it depends a great deal on the sort of facilities you can install into your backyard or your shoot. Even if your family has been throning over the same stately pile for centuries, they may not like your shots ripping into the tonsured

J.D.'s shooting partner, Neil, practising on pieces of chalk on the Downs.

turf of the putting green.

In a small garden you may only have enough length for a decent range in one direction even if it means standing at the back of the living room and firing the length of the garden through the French windows, as I do – after banning the dog and warning friends, family and guests. The easiest way to make a range is to get a four foot by three foot piece of chipboard, thick plywood, or planking and make a permanent back-stop using posts driven into the ground. With a metal target holder set just above the middle, you'll have a perfectly safe range. Without a target holder, the pellets ultimately punch right through the wood, rendering it dangerous. However, remember that your neighbour might become unnerved by a continuous stream of pellets thudding into the bull while he's trying to weed the garden or catch that elusive sun-tan.

Take care when firing towards blind corners, hedges and fences. Fences in particular can inspire a false sense of security, especially those made from wooden planks. Most hunting rifles are quite capable of punching through these brittle, thin, weathered laths of wood, much to the anguish of the aforementioned neighbour. It won't seem so funny when you find two policemen at the front door. Unsafe shooters had better think about taking out insurance. Damage claims can be ruinous – a house for an eye, a grand for a tooth!

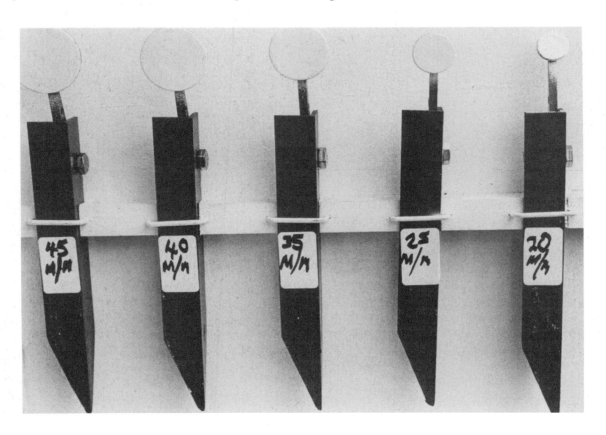

Simple knock-down targets like these are ideal for your brief daily practice sessions.

*The knock-down target, and cheap ammunition, enable shooters to
spend hours in enjoyable practice.*

You don't have to buy targets, you can use cardboard from cornflakes packets with several marker-pen dots to sight on. You obliterate them one after the other, or until the target becomes so riddled that it falls to pieces. You can't shoot more cheaply than that. Some people make a range out of a large cardboard box stuffed with rags, packed straw or paper to catch the pellet. The target is either a mark on the side or a paper square stuck on with sticky tape. This is certainly quieter than a wooden back-stop and metal holder. It is also a little safer. One of the problems with hard wood is that the pellet sometimes comes whanging straight back at the shooter. Normally it is tumbling so fast that you can hear the whine. Shooting glasses or sunglasses will protect your eyes against accidents. They're certainly more capable of fielding a spent pellet than a naked eyeball.

Paper targets aren't very interesting, though. Thankfully there are alternatives. A decoy crow, duck, or pigeon, with its hollow plastic body packed with rags to stop the pellets, makes a good mark. There are rigs on the market that let you haul the thing back into position on its pole with a string, ready for the next shot.

The knock-down target works on a similar principle. While the plastic pigeon

Compared to other shooting sports, accuracy comes cheap with air rifles, as this display of knock-down targets shows.

has pride of place on the pool shoot at field target events, it's the knock-down target which has caused the biggest stir, greatly increasing the opportunities to shoot with air weapons and adding to their popularity.

The target is a metal outline of a rat, rabbit, squirrel, pigeon, crow or whatever you fancy. There's a hole in the heart area – a natural killing zone – with a metal plate behind. Hit this, and a simple catch is released, causing the target to fall flat. A good yank on a stout string and the target sits up ready for the next shot, obviating the need to stalk wild critters for target practice. These targets must be securely pegged down, though, or the firm yank on the string will drag them out of the ground.

Some people club together and set up permanent layouts at different ranges in the woods. At one club on the Mendip hills I was shown a knock-down grizzly bear. Only the head was hinged, but it hit the body with a tremendous bang. A couple of knock-downs in the back garden could be fun, although for my money I prefer a spinning target. There's no need to yank on a string.

This is a rectangular metal hoop that you stick into the ground in front of your back-stop. On the rung is a blade that is trapped in the middle by collars. The blade has one flange heavier than the opposite one, and on to this you can stick little self-adhesive fluorescent targets. Hit this flange, and you'll hear a lovely smack and the blade will spin round and round, dissipating the transferred energy. The smack normally signals the complete shattering of the pellet against the blade's inertia.

At other times there are all those impromptu targets you can use to practise your marksmanship – fungi, leaves, conkers, apples, dandelions, pine-cones, old golf balls – practically anything.

A knock-down grizzly bear – every club should have one.

However, I don't think it is fair to fire into trees – apart from the occasional shot or maybe a bit of sighting in on a weedy maple sapling that nobody wants anyway. Mature trees are respected by all countrymen. Besides, heavy wounding will attract parasites and allow wind-blown diseases to penetrate the tree's defences.

Another trick that some shooters play, but which is totally dumb, involves firing at the caps of live twelve-bore cartridges. This is extremely dangerous. The cartridge won't go off as you expect when you hit the cap. Instead, the cap itself will fly out of the base of the cartridge at about twice the speed as the pellet came out of your rifle. I know somebody who tried

A few cheap silhouette targets like these can be laid out to form a permanent range in the garden.

this trick. He said it was like being shot in the face. He's coping with blindness quite well.

But there is one game you can play, although shooting glasses are a must to protect your eyes. I place caps for toy guns, and red match-heads along the little sill between my garage floor and the concrete driveway. It's only an inch deep – a long concrete corner. It takes quite some marksmanship at ten yards, but the bang when you hit is worth every miss. And once you get the measure of your mark, there will be strings of bangs. Just remember the glasses because the pellet is blown back at you, albeit feebly, by the blast.

Another target idea you may have space for is the running target. Preferably you should have a back-stop that's five yards long and high enough to completely cover

the little target sliding along its runners across the target area. It is possible to make a running boar (or stag, rabbit, rat and so on) range in your garden. Really it is essential to practise on moving targets if you plan to go hunting. Moving live quarry is difficult to hit and there is also the risk of wounding. Only practice and experience can eliminate this risk, just as they help in the early days when sitting targets are equally as hard to hit.

Not that you need a running boar range – a brisk stream and a good supply of leaves, corks, bits of plastic foam or whatever will help you to hit trotting bunnies. Once you get the knack, it'll enable you to tackle some difficult shots with both confidence and mastery.

It seems that some hunters have a mental aversion to shooting at paper targets. I can get my rifle to freeze motionless in my hands when I'm targeting a live thing, but how I hate watching that bull's-eye bouncing around in the sight. Paper lacks the urgency and excitement of live quarry. This is why plinking offers more interesting and varied shots – always provided that they are safe.

Live Quarry

The ultimate aim of it all is to be able to kill cleanly when you need to. We all owe it to our quarry simply out of care for other living things. No matter what the quarry, aim for the head, neck or heart. Hits in these areas will be lethal and misses unlikely to wound. The body always looks big and tempting, but not only does a shot there risk spoiling excellent meat; it is also criminally unfair on your quarry. There is a high risk of it being badly wounded, but escaping to die.

Very often it is essential to wait until your quarry presents itself better for a

Hunters are rarely able to fire in such a comfortably composed position when out after game. This is a field target shooter.

Many a woodpigeon's life has been saved by tiny twigs like these.
Even though they're puny, they can still deflect a pellet.

telling shot. Provided there's little chance of them spooking, the rabbit will quite probably hop out from among the brambles, the pigeon will turn around and waddle along its branch, presenting you its breast, and the squirrel will edge further away from the screen of twigs, inviting a smack in the head.

There are plenty of occasions when a haze of twigs, leaves or grass obscures your quarry. If you try to fire through it, the pellet will probably be deflected. The ricochet may not go whining away across the sky, but you'll certainly miss. Some-

times there'll be only enough room for your line of sight, but none for the pellet. Be patient. Maybe you can circle round a bit or wait until it presents a better view. Even if you don't get a shot this time, a better opportunity will come another day, bringing total satisfaction.

Once I was stalking rabbits on the far side of a wire fence with heavy grass growing along the bottom. After poking the barrel through the grass, and taking careful aim on a bunny less than ten yards away, my certain shot produced a startling shriek of a ricochet. The line of sight looked clear, but a strand of wire was stretched scant inches in front of the muzzle. Always make a check for grass, twigs and wires that you might not have seen because they were out of focus in the scope.

Frequently it is vital to keep the quarry in the sights, especially a squirrel that is hopping from branch to branch, or a rabbit that is creeping between the tussocks. This is where muscle control bears fruit, enabling you to watch for your opportunity. The squirrel or rabbit will suddenly pause. Your cross-hairs will be there, with your micro-missile doing its

damage even before you think about it. This is reflex shooting at its best.

My preferred free-standing stance, with the rifle locked by my shoulders, is excellent for taking moving shots. There is nothing difficult about them. Often your quarry will be moving, and if it is moving across in front of you, like a slow rabbit in the lamplight, the only opportunity for a shot may be by swinging the rifle.

Airgun pellets are much slower than those from a shot-gun, so quite a few inches of 'lead' are required. It is always best to perfect this technique on the running boar range first. Such a tactic teaches

Where accuracy is its own reward, and practice pays off.

the basic principles so that when a perfect crossing shot presents itself, you'll have it in you to make it work. Lead is the amount of space you put between your quarry and your line of sight before you squeeze the trigger. The rifle needs to be kept swinging.

When that bunny runs for cover, shoulder the rifle, swing with the cross-hairs on its head, then give the rifle a little push past its nose and squeeze off when you're about six inches past it. Obviously a huge amount depends on rifle, range and all the other variables. Fortunately, as a sports photographer, I have to use a similar technique to get some of my pictures.

About the best reward that airgunners can get from their sport is that warm, smug feeling that comes after succeeding with a tricky shot. Marksmanship must be a developing skill if it is to continue to satisfy. Even so, I'll never forget the feeling of near disbelief that came over me after I took my first killing shot at a bolting bunny. It was one of a pair that lived on the edge of an old Bronze Age hill-fort. The big ditch has filled in, but the bank allowed me to creep up and find them feeding where thatched huts once stood.

They both treated me like an invader and ran for cover every time my lamp appeared over that earthen rampart. But, one time, one of them dithered just a little too long and paid the price. It was many trips later, on an appalling night with a gale sweeping over the Downs, that I found the buck way out from cover. I walked straight at him, and realising his vulnerability he crouched in the short grass. The gale was banging at my body, rattling the rifle in my grasp. My shot flew wide – taken nervously at a ridiculous range – and the rabbit started running towards me. I reloaded fast. He stopped, feeling cut off from cover by my lamp. He was so near, but I fluffed the shot and missed again. Again he took to his heels while I, angry at myself, banged another pellet into the breach. I'll show you, I thought, swinging the rifle on to him like a shot-gun. I instinctively squeezed when the sight-picture looked right, but didn't notice that he was just about to vanish behind a tussock.

He didn't appear out the other side. Perhaps the wraith of a Bronze Age warlord had touched my trigger because my bunny lay stretched out, dead in its tracks, cleanly shot through the heart.

6 Hunting Techniques

One factor alone makes a puny weapon like an air rifle effective in the hunting field, and that's woodcraft. Without it, you'll be unable to get close enough to wild animals without arousing their natural reluctance to end up on a plate. It may be sporting among rimfire rifle shooters to take quarry at long ranges, but then these weapons are capable of such performance. Their bullets can fly the distance and still be full of destructive energy for a hard-hitting kill; but not an air weapon.

Our little pellets simply run out of energy too soon. This reduces their effective range considerably, necessitating close-range shooting. Sometimes people brag about making kills at sixty or seventy yards. Maybe they do, but the risk isn't fair. Airgun ammunition retains so little shocking power at such ranges that even accurate shooting leads to wounding. One feels compelled to ask how much injured game escapes for each successful long shot?

Know Your Quarry

I'm always impressed by countrymen who can fix it so they get up close to their quarry. It isn't so hard to do, either. The trick is to study the habits of wild animals, their likes and dislikes. It soon becomes apparent that each wild thing has a taste which you can exploit – decoying pigeons to a stubble field, for example. Alternatively, there's a chink in their natural wariness which can be developed – as

with lamping rabbits on an autumn night.

The intimate details of your quarry's habits aren't easy to come by. Such knowledge is learned only after spending numerous hours creeping around the countryside and skulking behind bushes, doing nothing more than observing. Country walks are an excellent way to get to know how wild creatures behave, especially early and late in the day when they're most active. While out on my walks I often discover a tree that has become fashionable as a look-out post for crows, or a crop of wild berries which the pigeons have found. Later that evening while the crows and pigeons are roosting, I'll be weaving my little hide tight into a handy thorn-bush. The place won't be so popular by sundown tomorrow.

It is important to be able to read the body language of wild creatures. See heads raised in alarm, or sunk contentedly into the shoulders. Watch how they react not just to you and your passing, but to other events. Note how the pigeon, although not alarmed, continually turns his eye to the lane at the bottom of the hill where a couple of people are walking.

Even when you're travelling around you'll notice little things, particularly how the habits of wild creatures change with weather and season. This continuous awareness of your quarry will soon provide a sound working knowledge of how you should behave in its presence. You'll know that when a woodpigeon's head comes up and stares hard in your direction, it may be more than natural wariness checking out the situation. Freeze while the eyes are staring, no matter how odd the stance. When you're no longer the object of a suspicious gaze, get into cover as carefully as possible. You may not think you've been spotted, but that sharp stare was provoked by something. Was it a sudden flash of pink face as you peered for a better look? Perhaps an over-hasty movement caught its eye? Did you cross a thin shaft of sunlight filtering through the woodland leaves? Was there a cracking twig? A magpie or crow will already be gone; a pigeon will mark the spot and keep it under surveillance. It'll give you enough rope to hang yourself, or for you to outwit it.

You don't need to tote a rifle on all your trips, indeed you'll not be allowed to shoot in some places. Still, that doesn't prevent you from watching, and sometimes a pair of binoculars will ultimately put more into the bag. Close observation shows you where to site hides and also enables you to plan stalking routes. You can lie out on the hill on a summer evening and note the routes rabbits take from their warrens and where gaps in the bushes allow you to creep right up to them. These points are often not readily discovered by wandering around the shoot itself. Indeed, long-distance observation is probably the only effective way to discover the flight lines that wood-pigeons use between their roosts, feeding points and watering holes.

I spend a lot of time photographing field sports for magazines. This work takes me to grouse moors and pheasant coverts, to opening meets and lurcher shows, and while I enjoy the wit and sophistication of professionals, I find it sad that so many can spend a day afield

When stalking, it's often best to set out for a predetermined place from which to take the shot.

and remain so totally blind to all the little things that are happening around them – the flight of curlew before the grouse come skimming over the purple shag-pile; the tree-creeper working the tall oaks for insects while pheasants rocket over-head. These guys so often lack the keen involvement with nature's patterns that separates them from true countrymen.

A countryman observes – it's second nature. That's why most of them are so good with dogs, as they don't need words to understand clearly what is going on in their heads and how to respond to their needs. In the hunting field it is essential to be able to read the state of mind of your quarry, and you can do this easily by watching its eyes and body movements. You can practise this in the pub too. As a species we humans are about four million years old, and still we communicate for much of the time with grunts and odd noises. Likewise, everybody is the inno-cent product of their background and you can read this quite clearly by watching how their faces respond to the changing situations and topics of conversation that swirl and eddy around every local.

A countryman can see with a glance at the sky what many people can't see on a weather map. Years in wild places teach how the cloud formations and winds change with good and bad conditions. Around my part of the world, close by the sea, I may not get too excited by a forecast for a good breeze on a night when I have planned to go lamping. Because I spend so much time fishing, I like to keep in constant contact with the weather map, watching the fronts cross the Atlantic or swirl up from the Continent. Maybe I'll have seen the most recent forecast after the six o'clock news, which promises a breeze. But outside, the night is still and frosty, and low tide isn't until eleven o'clock. In this part of the world, a rising wind comes with a rising tide, the two

turning together almost as regular as clockwork. I need wind to cover the sound of my approach, and the rise in temperature will thaw the grass and bring out the bunnies. But the breeze will come too late to make it worth going out, because there's work to be done tomorrow.

Hides

One of the best ways to observe wildlife is from a hide. Indeed, anybody with an interest in photography would be advised to take along a camera, tripod, and the biggest telephoto lens you can find. If you site your hide in the right place you'll be presented with plenty of species which are on the protected list. If your hide is effective, you may have only to pan the camera on its tripod to end up being nominated wildlife photographer of the year.

Most wild animals spend much of their time making sure they don't end up as prey. This means that only youngsters have the natural curiosity, or plain stupid-ity, to check out something that arouses their suspicion. In the autumn, when so much young and inexperienced game is around, you don't need to be so careful. At other times of the year, however, wild things steer well clear of anything out of the ordinary.

Perhaps you go shooting every Satur-day morning. The countryside always looks roughly the same, except for the changing of the seasons. To the wildlife, though, the woods and fields are as fami-liar as your living-room. When you're observed building a confused pile of vegetation in the middle of their living-room, they will become so concerned that they vacate the place.

This sort of hide can work, however, provided it is built as a permanent fixture.

Shooting from a hide. Denser cover is required for crows, who noticed the author moving against the skimpy background.

The problem is that leaves droop and die, so the next time you visit you'll have to disturb it all again by thickening up the bald patches. The wildlife may have got used to the fixture by then, though. They'll sit at the far end of the wood, far out of range, giving you a boring and frustrating day.

The first consideration when building a hide is choosing a site. This decision is based on one factor: where your quarry is. Quite a lot of research is necessary before you can be sure precisely where to build. Ideally it will be sited with a full field of view out front, and preferably without much chance of game appearing behind you. It is much easier to watch over a 180 degree field of view than to keep twisting round and round to observe all directions.

I suppose that under these circumstances two people could share a hide, but not sitting back to back. Face each other, keeping barrels well to either side, then you can chat quietly until game arrives. Make sure you arrange and both understand a safe shooting routine, though.

Remember that wind direction can affect which end of a wood the pigeons fly into. Notice that the breezes close to the ground may eddy into the prevailing wind, taking your scent to those rabbits upwind. Range is a most important consideration, too. Unless your potential site is in the open, just sit and watch what goes on for an hour or two. Leave the rifle at home, but wear full camouflage and keep still. You'll be spotted, for sure, and will spook plenty of game, but you'll be able to tell the potential of the place by the frequency with which visitors drop by.

If it's busy, it promises a good hunt. This final, inert observation will also tell you if the hide would be best sited twenty yards to your right. After all, with a maximum effective range of fifty yards on the smallest game, and about half that for big quarry like rabbits, the siting of a hide has to be as precise an operation as zeroing a scope. However, once you have fully evaluated the potential of your shoot, you'll find several sites which you can rely on at different seasons, year after year. Often you'll notice opportunities to exploit brief situations which occur when wild creatures, themselves arch opportunists, find a locally abundant food supply, for example. With this in mind, it's worth keeping up with the farm manager's plans, perhaps ambushing pigeons after sowing or on the day a field is harvested.

Within a day or two of your visit, the wildlife will have forgotten all about your intrusion. Now's the time to weave your lair. There aren't many places where the natural vegetation happens to be just right for an instant hide. Most times, the old ivy tree that falls into the cleft of another, providing dense cover underneath, lies about fifty yards from the centre of the action, making it quite unsuitable for anybody but spectators.

Think of a hide as a cocoon that conceals you from prying eyes. It should be no larger than is strictly necessary to allow you freedom of movement. The bigger your hide, the more it risks being noticed and the more cover you'll need to weave into it. Most times you'll be sitting; although if the hide needs to be sited in the open, think about lying flat out, rolling over on to your back to relieve the inevitable stiffness and aches.

The best basis for a hide is a camouflage net. There are two types: one comes with lengths of scrim (a sort of hessian bandage usually dyed brown or green) woven through it; the other has plastic panels of imitation scrim stapled along it. These solid panels are much more obvious than the random stippling of scrim. My preference is for the scrim net, although it is more bulky and heavier. For a start there's no rustling plastic. Another reason is that plastic-covered nets don't come very big, unlike the former type. Your choice may be governed by availability. Whichever type you settle on, give it a few good tramples in the mud or leave it on the bare earth of the vegetable patch for a few months. This weathers the material, causes dyes to run, and mud to streak. The colours will be subtly mellowed.

Because my net is on the large side, I can increase its density by doubling it. This adds to the shagginess of its outline. Set it in place by sitting in your hide and working from the inside, arranging it so that you can fire through it unobstructed, keeping it as small as possible. Places to set up are along the bottom of fences (even open, barbed-wire ones), under bushes, among the roots of trees – anywhere that you can dress it up to look like a natural extension of an existing part of the landscape. But it must be an unobtrusive extension.

The value of net is that bits of vegetation can be woven into it, concealing the fact that it's scrim-covered mesh. This final touch will make or break a hide. You don't want large bits of material. Neither do you want vegetation that is going to wilt and droop suspiciously under a hot summer sun. Many plants have leaves which are a different colour underneath. If you show this as part of your hide, wild creatures won't fail to notice it.

My preference is for thistles because they're so tatty anyway. Even though they don't cover well, by using enough I can build an invisible hide on the edge of a

An unobtrusive hide woven into a hawthorn bush.

field. In woodland, many different plants are suitable, particularly evergreens. It all depends on where you are and what's available.

The final effect is of a shaggy little cocoon without a definite outline. You'll have allowed for clear viewing and shooting, but don't forget to make the backdrop really thick. Otherwise, when you move, wild animals will see a shadowy movement inside the hide as your silhouette covers the little chinks of light coming in from behind.

Even when you're in a hide it pays to wear full camouflage and to keep the areas of pink skin under cover just in case wild creatures spot your movements through your viewing and shooting holes. Never shoot over the top of your hide, except when using a shot-gun on flying birds. With an air rifle, concealment at close range is of paramount importance, so shoot through it whenever possible.

Comfort is important for a long day in a hide. Because you can't move much circulation becomes sluggish, and even on a hot summer's day a shady hide is a cold and draughty place to be. In winter you'll need a whole wardrobe full of thermal clothing and moon boots to keep warm; and not much less in high summer. Draughts are more of a problem in winter, although they are inevitable in summer, too. You can site hides to minimise

The author weaving thistles into a camouflage net to create a hide.

Even the skimpiest of backgrounds enforces the effect of camouflage clothing.

this. Under extreme conditions you may feel the need to incorporate an internal wind-break. Use a sheet of drab plastic material, an old groundsheet, or something similar. Don't use polythene because it's impossible to tie and peg it sufficiently tightly to prevent it from flapping irritatingly. A cushion is an essential part of ambushing, preventing a numb bum, pins and needles, and all those discomforts that are a consequence of sitting for hours on cold, hard ground.

When it's really cold or you're hunting the fields, you may prefer to build a hide from straw bales. These really are snug, and you can use one to sit on. You need about a dozen to complete such a mansion. However, they're most effective outside harvest time when they have been allowed to weather. An orange coloured straw hut in the middle of a black, winter wood will be noticed, and probably shunned, by everything. Let it weather for half a year and it'll look quite different. It may turn out to be an excellent permanent hide.

You don't always have to build a hide to ambush game. Sometimes you can sink into a bush or behind a clump of nettles within perfect range of activity. At other times you'll find that a vantage point from a bough up in a tree will be quite adequate for a productive session. This applies particularly to rabbits, because a tree lifts your scent above ground level, making you undetectable. For some reason wild animals rarely look up. I would have thought that aeons of being attacked by hawks and eagles would have made those creatures more wary of attacks from on high. It isn't the case, though, so we may as well exploit the blind spot.

Another blind spot, literally, is the inability of all of us to see into deep shadow when the sun is bright. You need only to wear full camouflage and hide your face and hands to become totally invisible to everything out in the field. If you can arrange it so that your quarry has

to look directly into the sun to see you, there's absolutely no need for a full hide. A solid background, however, is essential. Sometimes you can stalk rabbits out of the sunset, but they must be in the sunlight and you must try to creep below it, watching that your shadow doesn't go near them. It feels odd to crawl down a hill towards rabbits that stare straight at you, then carry on feeding. Sometimes you can get within twenty yards.

Decoying

Hide making and decoying are skills that complement one another. Having studied

A fallen tree makes a good hide for rabbits, as they rarely look up.

your quarry and learned how to fool it in one way, a few decoys add an additional level of deceit to your plans. Close observation will have taught you much about how the movements of your quarry vary according to the time of day. It is sensible to build a hide in a roost when the birds have gone to feed.

Decoying applies almost exclusively to birds. Birds have the mobility to travel long distances each day, so whether they're roosting, resting, drinking or feeding they'll provide a variety of opportunities for interception.

You can buy a variety of plastic birds, especially woodpigeons. Some are designed to be set out on fences and branches, others are for use among crops or in freshly drilled fields. Some sit still, some flap naturally, and others flap when you tweak a string. The best decoy of all is a live bird; but it's illegal to tether one. The next best thing is a dead bird. You can buy frames to clip around them and transform them into flappers. With their wings wide, pigeons expose the white bars that tell the incoming airborne that undisturbed feeding is going on below. By tweaking the string, the decoy flaps, like a bird hopping over others of the flock when a fresh feeding ground is discovered.

Dead birds can be frozen and used several times in cold weather until they're better left for the foxes. In hot weather, out on an exposed stubble field, the flies will have blown them with eggs before the day is out. The way to set up a dead bird is to lay it on its back, taking care not to damage its plumage, especially the white neck bands. Take your knife and insert the point into the cleft of its beak and force it into the skull. By doing this on the ground there's no risk of the knife slipping right through into the palm of your hand, making you the blood brother of a long-dead woodie. Twist the knife to

make a hole big enough for a long, thin stick.

Place the bird the right way up, head facing towards the wind, and poke the stick into the ground. It is intended to keep the head high and natural, making the bird look alive and attentive. Arrange the body with the wings tucked close in to the sides, the feet trailing astern. This is quite enough to have live birds waddling and feeding among your decoys without a care in the world, especially if you've put down a few handfuls of corn to keep them occupied.

There is a way of preserving pigeons by injecting them with formalin. A more convenient compromise is to take a plastic shell decoy and attach real wings flat on to the sides with wires. There's something about the texture of feathers which plastic and paint can't match, and this compromise, when made to look natural, is as effective as anything else.

The birds themselves will tell you where to put your decoys. When field shooting, they need to be close to you, possibly with the killing zone right in the middle. Pigeons love to belong to flocks, they feel more secure that way. The decoyer ensures that his layout provides a nicely situated gap for new arrivals to drop into. Remember that they alight facing the wind.

Decoys can readily be mounted high in trees by the use of a catapult and fishing line. Tie a stone or a lump of lead to the end of some 20lb line and, with the nylon coiled over the ground and the far end tied down, fire the missile over a chosen branch. Now tie one end to the front, the other to the back, of a plastic decoy and hoist it over the branch. To prevent it being blown off by the wind, tie a big stone or a weight to the lower loop of nylon, letting it hang a few feet above the ground beneath the decoy. The branch can bounce all over the place in the wind, but your decoy will stay put. If the tree isn't too tall, you should be able to throw a missile by hand over a chosen branch.

Decoys should never appear to droop, as that's a dead give-away. It's often the reason why decoys on fence posts don't work. Good decoys here are great for attracting woodies to cattle drinking troughs, but it's hard to mount them at the right angle. If this turns out to be a problem, fit a stiff wire frame inside the bird, leaving long ends to wrap around posts and along the topmost strand of the fence. Under such conditions, results will be better if you can bunch the birds a bit. They must also be sufficiently secure to withstand the twang of a real live bird landing on the fence. It doesn't look good if your decoys one by one slump upside-down like pie-eyed parrots on a perch.

Another method of decoying involves quite a different tactic. Instead of encouraging birds to come around with promises of food and security, it sometimes pays to aggravate them. This is particularly appropriate to the crow family – the corvids. The trick is to find out where crows and magpies meet to discuss the world and, before they arrive, set up a decoy of a small owl. You can buy flappers, and really stir them up. You'll find more on this in Chapter 11.

Good hides frequently come ready-made.

Whatever type of decoying you get into, the important rule is to make them stand out clearly without looking unnatural. That's quite an art.

Other tricks attract game within range – you can bait some species and call others. A combination of decoys and calls, in practised hands, brings ducks within shot of even an air rifle. Some countrymen can call hares.

Liberal daily applications of grain to a quiet corner of a field attract pigeons, doves and other game within range. Stake out a dead rabbit with its innards exposed and you'll attract magpies and crows galore. Observe the birds out foraging and study the beats that they patrol.

Stalking

In my opinion, stalking is a much more direct test of skill than decoying. You have to rely on your wits to work ever-changing situations to your advantage. This particularly applies when you have a specific bird or animal to stalk. Then the sport reduces to terms of one against one – success or failure. A stalk may take half an hour to accomplish. After spending this amount of time creeping and watching, sneaking closer and closer without being spotted, the concluding moment arrives. It is most satisfying when the final tweak of the trigger is met by the loud crack of lead against bone. The tougher the stalk, the more rewarding the kill.

To stalk well you have to be able to move over the ground like a spirit, attracting scant interest in your passing. The technique comes quickly if you're mercilessly self-critical on woodland walks. One method of working a belt of cover is to drift through it, pausing for ten minutes or so every fifty yards to keep a check on what's going on round about. Experience tells where best to linger and where

you can walk quite openly.

Full camouflage is essential if a hunter is to spend time in the open. Often you'll have to freeze, maybe for minutes on end, while some wily critter eyes you suspiciously. However, you can make life easier for yourself by reducing the likelihood of this happening. Keep well within cover or the shadows, or at least within easy reach of them.

When you have to break cover, which is essential to get from one copse to another, you may as well walk across the open ground looking as nonchalant as possible. Wild animals can tell a furtive stance a mile off. They'll become more suspicious if you act like your presence in their backyard isn't entirely in their best interests. They also have an instinctive dislike to being stared at. Consider this.

Years ago there was a form of film advertising, now banned, in which a message was flashed up as one frame only, too quickly for the conscious mind to register it. But the subconscious could absorb it, and some people really did obey these hidden instructions to buy certain brands. To the bird or animal that you're staring at, your eyes are wide and clear to see, even from partial concealment. Two staring eyes may seem insignificant, like the single frame with a sales message, but the subconscious mind spots it. Like the pink face, two staring eyes on the front of the face are a human characteristic, albeit one that's shared by most predators. The creature feels uncomfortable. It feels spotted. Maybe it's time to move on. The hunter peeps through hooded eyes, carefully reading and recording the changing scene, then drops his gaze lest he offend.

The wind is a stalker's most fickle friend. Compared to the breeze, the lives of most wild creatures are simple and predictable routines. A hot, dry breeze carries scent badly, while a damp one brings out the smell of everything. Watch

84

Full concealment is not essential for rabbit shooting – scent and the wind direction are more important.

the smoke from a bonfire, how it drifts across the garden in a steady breeze, choking the neighbours. Light it on a windy day and you'll see how turbulence from trees, shrubs and fences breaks up the smoke, keeping it from some places, pushing it into others. Smoke shows how the breeze can carry your scent ahead of you, or push it far behind.

Most times it is best to stalk into the breeze, but you don't just need wind to create a current of air. Picture the rabbits on the hillside as the shadows lengthen towards evening. It has been a gloriously hot day, and the breeze is flowing sweetly over the hill towards you. With plenty of cover, a stalk seems a cinch. When you're

about a hundred yards away, a big old buck sits up straight, his eyes wide and staring. Then, thumping his foot in the stillness of the evening, he bumps off into the bushes. Soon the others are following; their white scuts flashing in the dying sunlight. They pause at the edge of the gorse, ready to dive for cover.

Bewildered, you look around searching for the cause. Maybe a vixen has started on her rounds, or somebody has brought his dog or a friend to enjoy the peaceful evening. No, it was none of these. With the dying of the sun, warm air from the valley began creeping up the hill, the natural convection after a hot day. That's why the bunnies were so taken by the sunset and why they scented you soon after you broke away from the path.

The cold air that flows into the valley has to come from somewhere. Probably it will move down from a higher valley or hillside that lost the sun's heat earlier in the evening. In my part of the world it flows in from the sea. Wherever the cold air comes from, you can feel it. Walk the hills after a hot summer's day and, if there's no wind, the air on the tops will be lovely and warm at midnight – ten degrees warmer than in the valleys. There, drifts of mist bear witness to the sliding currents of air.

The stronger a breeze, the more it swirls and eddies around objects in its path. Think of the wind as ricocheting off bushes and woods, and the stronger the wind, the more likely it is to rebound wildly. Even though a wind is coming over a field at right angles to you, a gust may push your scent right across it and therefore many yards up the hedge. However, sometimes you can get around swirling winds by rearranging your stalking routes.

Totally unpredictable, though, are winds caused by turbulence around hills and woods. They swirl first from one direction, then from another. A light breeze may be filtering through the wood, adding a third dimension to the problem. You must trust to luck under these circumstances, or stalk quarry which has a less discriminating sense of smell, like woodpigeon.

Stalking is all about getting close without being spotted. It is all very well to drift through the woods, scanning for quarry each time you pause to become an integral part of the countryside, but the real McCoy only comes about after you've spotted a potential target. To make matters more interesting it may be one of a group. Instead of just one pair of wary eyes, you have to avoid detection by

several. Animals watch each other's body language, and alarm signals are soon picked up by the group.

First, take careful note of intervening cover and any routine in your quarry's behaviour when there may be a lull in wariness – like when a rabbit drops his head to feed. Watch out for this, though it may be a trick to make you show your hand. Is he really that intent on chewing?

Use all available cover and slip through it, as soundless as a shadow. Trust that the breeze won't betray you. The closer you get, the more slow and considered your movements must be. You are that much more likely to fall foul of your quarry's defence systems. Maybe you have to cross an open space, using a stunted patch of nettles for cover. Lie flat, holding the rifle in your hands. Crawl on your elbows, knees and toes. Don't drag your body, it makes too much noise. Take your time – you have all you need until you make a mistake and your quarry becomes aware of you. Ideally this never happens. You must be silent and invisible so that your quarry is unaware of you right up until it is dead.

Take a slow peep out from beneath your eyebrows, keeping your head low. Is it still there, as contented as before? Careful now, lower your head, gingerly slip forward like a cat closing for its kill. Your muscles may scream with the strain. Rest a moment, take it easy. Do nothing to spook your quarry. Finally you're there, well within range. Maybe it'll yawn or scratch, as if to let you know that nothing in particular is bothering it right now. Slowly, oh so slowly, raise the rifle to your shoulder, careful lest a sudden movement attracts interest. Now dodge your head behind the scope, consider the technicalities of the shot, and place the cross-hairs on your mark.

Even before you take the shot you'll feel a warm glow of certainty as though

Shadows and scant cover are often all a hunter needs to conceal himself.

the stalk is already over. The slick squeeze of the trigger is almost a formality, albeit a telling one. So don't blow it now! Take the shot like it's the hardest you've ever fired. Over-confidence and hasty shooting cause plenty of misses.

Improving Your Shoot

A few seasons on a shoot soon teach the best routes to walk for effective stalking. These will be dictated by all the factors that enable you to move about undetected, allowing you to come up on your quarry unexpectedly. Sometimes it may prove worth your while to take a pair of secateurs and prune stalking rides through heavy cover, permitting access to popular roosts and concealed warrens. A rake will sometimes prove useful to clear away masses of dead leaves and twigs, allowing you to walk silently on bare earth rather than crunchily like you're stalking through a bowl of cornflakes.

How you cope with frozen conditions is up to you. With the landscape as scrunchy as icing sugar, stalking is practically out. If you have found places to build permanent hides, or even high seats, then a snowy day is as good as any to spend in one. This is assuming that the area covered by such a hide is attractive to game in severe weather.

Many people landscape their shoots in little ways that make them more attractive to birds and animals. For example if you plant food crops like sweetcorn, you'll attract all sorts of birds to feed on the kernels. This idea is used on many pheasant estates. A ten yard wide belt of food and cover running the length of a wood does wonders to keep pheasants from wandering. Your patch will attract pigeons for sure, and also any pheasants that stray in from neighbouring areas.

It must be many centuries since the last proper warren was built; although humans often create cosy homes for rabbits, particularly among rubbish dumps. One of my favourite stalks is to a warren which exists solely because a bomb crater was filled with rubbish. The brave Luftwaffe left plenty of these craters around the Sussex Downs. Some gallant aviators didn't wait until the Spitfires were upon them before jettisoning their bombs to speed their escape. Most of these little hollows now have warrens around the rim.

You can achieve the same if you have a pile of broken concrete to get rid of or some old railway sleepers and the use of private land. Find a dry hollow, preferably on an open hillside facing the sun. Fill it with rubble, then cover as much of it as possible with polythene before topping it off with soil. If bunnies are scarce in your parts, ask a friend with a ferret for some live rabbits to introduce there. While colonisation takes place, plant gorse, blackberry and hawthorn bushes, and other suitable shrubs to serve as fire points and stalking cover later.

There are many other ways in which a shoot can be improved. It may even be wise for you to become a member of the Game Conservancy at Fordingbridge in Hampshire. Their teams of experts can advise on all types of game management. They know how to improve shooting amenity without getting a farm manager's back up. They may even persuade him to be less rapacious with his farming efficiency and not plough right up to the hedge roots.

7 Quarry, The Law and Safety

The hunter has a paradoxical relationship with his quarry. On the one hand he studies, encourages and cares for wild creatures, and on the other hand he kills them. You have really to get straight in your own mind what you consider to be legitimate quarry. This goes further than merely observing the law and sparing songbirds. Why shoot sparrows, for example, or starlings? They're both great comedians that have added plenty of additional interest to my moments outdoors.

Sure, I've shot or trapped plenty; but nowadays I see little point in extinguishing their lives for no reason, even though there's no shortage of them. After all, they don't bother many people. Sparrows can be an intense nuisance in thatched roofs, but their mischief has yet to be directed at me. Perhaps a proper covering of wire mesh on the roof would be more appropriate than sniping at the birds. This, though, is my own moral line.

There has to be a reason to take a life. This is the logic that resolves the delicate balance between both sides of that paradox. Life has a sanctity which every countryman respects. To take a life flippantly is loutish. It is this reason alone which has given air rifles a bad name. In the past, kids were not aware of how precious our wildlife is. The blackbird with a leg smashed by a pellet advertises its disability throughout the neighbourhood. Nine times out of ten everybody will be right to suspect an air gun. However, it would be nice to think that the abundance of wildlife programmes on the television has opened the minds of louts to the magnificence of the wild world. Blackbirds may not be the most glamorous of birds, nor are they found in the media-favoured South American Jungle; but they're just as interesting as all those exotic creatures, if you care to study them.

I have scant pity for predators like crows and magpies which, in most suburban gardens, destroy about eighty per cent of the first clutches of songbird eggs. The second clutch is more successful, because by July the cover is at its thickest. Woodpigeons are thought to be fair game by everybody; although they're actually quite scarce in many places. There has been a surge of interest in woodie decoying among shot-gun shooters. It seems from what I read that the sole criterion for a good day's sport is the weight of the sack afterwards. I'm amazed by the innocence of those letters in the shooting press enquiring where the woodies have all gone. They've been shot, mate. Over-shot. Just as the fish in the sea have been over-fished.

Still, there are plenty of woodies in other places, and if you are a gardener you'll know all about the damage that just one pair can do to a plot of peas. Whole rows of young vegetables have their growing shoots pecked out. No gardener likes to find his efforts sabotaged by a bird with a marked taste for the fat of the land. That's probably why they taste so good. I don't often spare woodies, unless they're very young. It's only fair they should live a bit, grow a bit more wily, become a more worthy mark. But this is one of several species which have been labelled 'vermin' and those numbers sometimes need to be kept in check.

Originally, man hunted for food, and this is still the best reason for doing so. I eat quite a lot of what I shoot, or give it to appreciative friends. My rabbit-seeking missile, the most beautiful lurcher in the world, lives almost exclusively on the bunnies we catch and shoot. Nothing will make me renounce my pleasure in eating the things that I shoot. The flavour is always superior to the meat that factory farming produces. The levels of chemicals, preservatives and cholesterol are very much reduced.

I'm told that the Italians produce an excellent pickled starling. The Italians, however, shoot and pickle everything that flies, thereby eradicating wildlife en masse from large tracts of countryside. Theirs is a silent spring.

Whatever you shoot, make sure that you are so familiar with it that you could never mistake it for any other species. 'I thought it was a pigeon,' will fall on deaf ears when countrymen are around. How could anybody confuse a rock-dove with a pigeon? Why, you have only to watch how they fly, and look at those ruby-red eyes and the dark collar.

It is every hunter's duty to follow up

Where most of us started – potting starlings around the garden.

Sparrows in the farmyard are a legitimate quarry – but hardly for the serious hunter.

wounded creatures lest they suffer a slow, painful death. Every effort must be made to retrieve hit game, including rats. Even greater efforts should be made to ensure that your marksmanship leaves scant chance of wounding.

Even a creature which you decide is fair game deserves a degree of respect. Humans have become very efficient at hunting and this poses a threat to some wild species.

Always be mindful that there's a limit to every resource and that some years the crop that you can take will be slight, or possibly non-existent.

There's another reason for not hammering wild animals. They don't take long to wise up to the threat you pose. After a time, birds will fly and squirrels will flee long before you can get within range. If you become too greedy, your

91

The starling, like all of Nature's food species, breeds abundantly and matures quickly.

stock of wild creatures will become so spooked that it moves elsewhere – and who can blame them. It's a risk that occurs when too little ground is available, and enthusiasm is a mite too high to allow acres to be rested between sessions.

However, circumstances differ according to locality. The thing to remember is that you'll ultimately make it harder on yourself if you make it too hard on your quarry. A large garden will support a reasonable shoot about once a fortnight. In between you'd be better advised to stick to discreet plinking. This doesn't mean that a pigeon strutting on the lawn isn't a fair mark. It's the repeated disturbance when animals want to feed or roost that drives them off.

Plenty of wild animals have legal protection nowadays, but the list of legitimate quarry species is more than adequate. Many of these you will never want to shoot at, while others are much too big to take out with an air rifle – even an air firearm. Because of the circumstances, a great deal depends on your own judgement of which species are permissible. I'll tell you the ones that I consider fair game. These include rabbits, grey squirrels, rats, mink, woodpigeons, feral pigeons, collared doves, carrion crows, hooded crows, rooks, magpies, and jays.

With an air firearm I have killed hares, foxes and feral cats upon request from landowners. However, even with such a powerful air rifle, shots have to be taken straight into the head and within twenty yards. An air firearm has double the power of a standard air rifle, so please don't even attempt to fire at this quarry unless you're so close that you're using the gun like a humane killer. Even then reflect on what you might be doing. The nape of the neck is the killing zone.

Sometimes a weasel or a stoat makes a nuisance of itself in the laying pen of a pheasant shoot. Such a rascal is best dealt with once and for all because it can do great damage, causing the keeper no end of headaches. Imagine what his boss would say if he knew that a stoat was making whoopee in the laying pen. Under these circumstances the air rifle solves the problem without scrambling all the unlaid eggs. Indeed, many pest control officers use them in built-up areas.

Young carrion crows offer vermin hunters the best opportunities in July.

Would you shoot this bird? Of course not – it's an immature blackbird. Quarry recognition is essential.

Their quietness and low power makes them unbeatable under such circumstances.

I know that jackdaws aren't the best loved of birds, but I like them and let them pass unhindered. I can't see any point at all in shooting some species from the quarry list, while others that are considered to be vermin don't bother me. I have no cause to persecute them. Some, like moorhens, are said to taste good; but I draw the line at rook pie.

There's a large chunk of the quarry list that shot-gun shooters would have you believe is their exclusive province. I'm referring, of course, to game birds: ducks, pheasants, partridges, snipe, woodcock, grouse, and so on. There is nothing in the law which states that you can only shoot these species with a shot-gun, even though some people would consider you as nothing better than a poacher. The game species make equally excellent marks for air rifle hunters. They really deserve a chapter on their own, though I anticipate that the many precepts and principles outlined in this book will enable you to make best use of every legitimate opportunity.

There are only two rules with regard to game shooting. First, consult with the land-owner, gamekeeper, or shoot captain. Be tactful and test the water cautiously before making outrageous propositions. Many landowners have scant interest in the game and will let you go ahead. Even on a sporting estate your marksmanship and shooting manners will not go unnoticed. You might be invited for a day out at the end of the season to thin the cocks a bit. I hope one day to go stalking grouse in Yorkshire. It strikes me that they present quite simple shots at times, while offering exacting challenges at others. Thus, by avoiding dim young things, I imagine ending the day with a bag containing maybe ten birds, each one an honour to the shot.

The second rule is to be ethical about what you shoot and how you shoot it. Respect the law, and any stipulations that are a condition of your access to the land.

Shoot game with an air rifle on some estates and you'll be branded as a poacher. Other landowners think differently.

The Law

Clear laws apply to the use of air weapons. You have to be 14 years of age before you can use one without supervision, and 17 before you can go into a shop and buy one.

You aren't allowed to shoot within close range of a public highway. It is quite illegal to shoot things at the roadside from a car. At no time may you shoot on any land, anywhere, without permission from the owner.

Silencers are not illegal, although some people have the false idea that they are.

The legal power limit for air weapons is 12ft lb of muzzle energy – in any calibre, with any ammunition, and under all

A collared dove – but a dangerous place to shoot it, in a built-up area.

circumstances. If you wish to hunt with an air firearm, you'll have to consult with your local police force. Strict guidelines affect the issue of a Firearms Certificate (FAC). In Northern Ireland an FAC is required prior to purchasing even a standard air rifle.

The law states that when you shoot in your garden, there should be no chance of shots straying or ricocheting outside it.

That's clear enough. Any shot that doesn't stop within your boundary is illegal and leaves you open to prosecution. Most neighbours are willing to allow a certain amount of disturbance, especially from an enthusiast who behaves responsibly. But once you overstep the bounds of courteous consideration, your activities will be resented. Be diplomatic.

It is also illegal to carry an air rifle in a

public place without it being covered by a fastened gun bag. This means you're not really allowed to cycle down the lane with your rifle over your shoulder; although your local bobby, if he knows you, will probably realise that you're no lunatic.

Always make sure that you know precisely which side of the fence your territory ends. The farmer's neighbour may be totally opposed to shooting. If you trespass, or are suspected of it, your presence will provoke such resentment between the two landowners that you'll lose your permission to shoot. That could be far more painful than missing the tempting rabbit that was sunning itself in the field on the far side of the hedge. You also risk ending up in court, which would be worse still.

When you get permission, hang on to it. A bottle of homemade sloe gin in the right hands at Christmas can do wonders for loyalty and encouragement. A birthday present is always a good idea too; but don't creep.

You have to remember that many different interests are combined into estate management. First there's the cropping: farming, forestry, and so on. Then come the sporting interests. Perhaps some areas have been reserved for wildlife conservation projects. Maybe tourists flock in their thousands. Possibly the landowner is a pillar of society and the Special Branch would rather not have camouflage-clad strangers slinking around the place.

At the bottom of the scale on most estates comes the airgun hunter. You'll have to fit in with all the other activities. Normally you will not be encouraged to shoot near farm buildings except when things are quiet at weekends. Some places may be off limits, as will some species. Maybe you'll be requested to phone ahead to arrange when would be convenient; although this is likely to be relaxed as your host gets to know and trust you better.

The major stumbling-block for most people is getting permission. Through my professional involvement with photographing and writing about fishing and field sports, I've got to meet lots of people. Offers of permission come without my asking, and I'm extremely fortunate to have several thousand acres of excellent shooting at my disposal. I guard these privileges jealously, anxious that my conduct should never be found wanting.

However, I used to be turned down time and time again. This was the result of too direct an approach. As soon as a landowner grants permission, he has something else to worry about. Imagine how he feels to be summoned by the doorbell from wrestling with the latest EEC Agricultural Directive only to find a fresh-faced lad cheerily asking if he can send lumps of lead whistling at high speed around his estate. The guaranteed result will be a firm, but polite refusal. Actually, anti-hunting farmers tend to be less polite, as they relish the opportunity to state their view unequivocally.

Stalk permission like you would a wily crow. Find out first whether the gamekeeper or the landowner is the man who has the say-so in such matters. Then find out what you can about whichever it is. Discover whether he visits the church or the pub; and when you feel fully briefed to take it a stage further, contrive to meet and have a chat with him. But don't mention hunting to start with. A time will come when you can tell him about your enthusiasm. Consider permission to shoot, which normally costs nothing to air rifle hunters, as the biggest game you can bag.

Ultimately the time will come when you can broach the question of permission, but not as a wild stab in the dark. The appropriate moment will arrive – possibly if he mentions that certain vermin are becoming a pest. Ask now. How about if you had a crack at them? – 'Gosh, what an excellent idea. You're sure you don't mind? When could you come up?' When the moment's right, getting permission is as easy as falling off a log. Time it badly, though, and you'll blow your chances for a long time. Even then, don't give up. Stalk your mark more cannily next time.

Farmers appreciate a helping hand at times, and gamekeepers also welcome offers to beat or help out. But don't think of doing this only with the ulterior motive of getting permission, it probably won't work. You have to show that you care for the countryside, and to demonstrate a thorough knowledge of how the ecology of an estate hangs together.

Safety

Everybody who shoots is extremely critical of the way other people handle guns. Most shooters pride themselves on observing meticulous safety routines. This is because safety comes only from safe habits. A small lapse can blind somebody, or even kill them. So never point an air rifle at anybody, even in fun. Fire to unload the rifle before taking on a tricky obstacle. This is better than breaking the barrel. If a twig catches the trigger, your rifle may suffer terminal damage. Never leave a rifle loaded or cocked when it isn't in use. That's both silly and dangerous, and how gun owners get themselves killed. I didn't know it was loaded, means nothing – you should never have pointed it in that direction.

This lesson was taught me by a rabbit. I was out lamping, spotted a bunny in the grass, and shot it through the head. When I got up to it, I saw another further off, also crouching in the grass. This I also shot, and reloaded, scanning for more.

The author's rifle balances perfectly when held like this, with the muzzle pointing safely at the ground while walking.

Seeing none, I laid the rifle beside the first rabbit using its white belly as a marker in the darkness, then walked to the second one. No sooner had I picked it up than the rifle went off. Fortunately it was facing away from me. The first rabbit's reflexes had started it jerking its hind legs. One had caught the trigger.

Mention of lamping brings to mind local by-laws, which vary around the country, especially with regard to night shooting. Check them out at the town hall; or if in doubt ask at the police station. Don't accept opinions – ask to see chapter and verse. Remember that some local councils have banned hunting on their land, including the allotments. If in doubt, shoot nowt and ask about.

Some people believe that no moving target should be attempted with an air rifle. This is to avoid wounding. However, an experienced shooter who practises this skill on the range is less likely to wound game than an inexperienced shooter who is still finding his way with sitting targets. Of course we should always prevent wounding, but that should not inhibit shooters from developing their skill to its highest limits. It should be emphasised that skill at moving quarry needs to be second nature on the range before it is applied to living quarry.

Consider this for a moment. A pigeon or a crow swaying in the breeze on the topmost branches of a tree is every bit as much of a moving target as a rat shambling along the bottom of a wall. The rightness of it is down to one factor – your own instinctive ability to execute such shots without so much as thinking about them.

8 Rabbits

My father taught me how to set a snare when I was seven and since that distant autumn day I've maintained an active interest in rabbits. This fast-breeding little animal swarms around the hills where I live, providing food and sport for myself and several dozen foxes. Indeed, a characteristic of all wild creatures that are eaten in abundance is that they mature and breed very quickly. Flies, sprats, mice and rabbits are regarded by large numbers of predators as convenience foods. I don't feel guilty for all the thousands of bunnies that have fallen to my wiles because they have all been put to good use.

Where to Hunt

Rabbits are most numerous on short grassland, like downs and dunes. They don't like too much cover because it allows foxes to ambush them when they return from their nights out in the fields. Warrens with a good view hold the largest numbers, especially where the grass is just tall enough to make good cover, but isn't so long as to conceal predators.

Woodland isn't so good, especially where warrens become waterlogged in winter. Banks are much preferred. Soil needs to be fairly crumbly and easily worked to encourage a thriving warren to develop. Around my part of the world, sandy bluffs have warrens of fifty or more holes, each one as big and open through centuries of use as the entrance to a stately home. These warrens are heavily used because of the short cover round about.

Woodland rabbits frequently have to run the gauntlet. Some are swamped by tall corn for part of the year, but find their food supply ploughed and inaccessible for several months at a time. They have to travel, and this nomadic life makes them vulnerable to predation.

Much depends on the type of cover. Bunnies prefer short stuff, like nettle beds, gorse and brambles. They riddle it with little tunnels, making a sort of ground-level sieve that strains out pursuers. Foxes and dogs can't penetrate it. They're checked while bunny carries on through, maybe at top speed. I work a lurcher and I was amazed in the early days at how rabbits make use of even the smallest feature to bring him to a stop. He has to accelerate again, thus giving them a few more yards to make it to cover.

Quite often one or two bunnies fancy themselves as champion sprinters – and they usually are. They feed hundreds of yards out in the field, and if the dog gets on to them, it is more than likely they'll escape by using one or two quite simple little obstacles. All they need is a few strands of wire – or a whole sheep fence, cattle drinking troughs, thistle beds, fallen branches, or the tiniest of bushes.

My wee dog in pursuit of a bunny once piled into a wooden seat fixed in concrete at the bottom of a steep hill, with a yelp and one hell of a thump. But, tough little critter that he is, he recovered quickly and it was the rabbit's turn to feel anxious. The two had come tearing down the hill straight into my lamp, and the rabbit was now totally dazzled. It was heading for a

The rabbit – a worthy and wary target for the air rifle hunter.

massive group of blackberry bushes, but the thick fronds were woven into tall grass, forming an impenetrable hedge. The rabbit checked, searching for a tunnel, and the dog smacked him with a vengeance.

Railway embankments are favourite places because the soil has been disturbed and is easier to tunnel. Indeed, you'll find that rabbits are quite capable of holding their own in all sorts of places – at motorway service stations, around industrial estates and airports, even in town parks.

There are two ways of going about getting rabbit shooting. One is to walk the ground you have available, looking for their signs: scratching, nibbled greenery, droppings, runs, and so on. Go to the same places at night with a lamp, especially if they're heavily disturbed by day, and you may be delighted at the number of bunnies out in the fields.

The other way is to find the places where their populations are highest, then try for permission to hunt there. It is fortunate that our little furry friend has such a bad reputation for multiplying in proportion to its food supply, taking every advantage of crops to do so. It doesn't rank very highly among game shooters, either. Rabbits are generally ignored on sporting estates during formal shoots, as there would be too much danger of hitting a beater. However, rough shooters find a bolting rabbit an exacting mark.

I have shared this delight myself. I used to creep along the hedgerows with a .410 magnum, shooting rabbits as they raced for cover from the fields. My best ever score was twenty bunnies with twenty cartridges – one miss, and two together with one shot. I do like it when one rabbit goes to overtake another just as I'm about to loose the shot. But I haven't handled a shot-gun for several years now. They make too much racket.

The increasing number of rough shooters is likely to limit your chances of getting permission, because these guys pay and the farmer will rightly point out that, having assigned the rights to a syndicate, he could face a legal backlash if he granted permission to you too. My favourite get-out was from an architect who also owns a farm. I used to meet him in the pub and he told me that if he granted permission, he might find himself being held liable for some accident that might befall me. But I don't mind you poaching it, he concluded. You might suggest this yourself, if you know the farmer well enough. It would be better to ask the syndicate boss, though.

When to Hunt

Rabbits are wary animals especially from late autumn onward. This makes them extremely worthy quarry for the stalker armed with an air rifle. At its best, stalking rabbits is very challenging. A wise rabbit has well-tuned instincts. Let no smell, sight or sense reveal your presence, and he is yours. It's a tough proposition. In some parts of the world, bunnies just love exposed hillsides.

Rabbits begin breeding in late January. As I'm not into pest control but would rather harvest a crop of young bunnies for the freezer, I don't indulge in too much shooting until the middle of August. In fact, as I grow more senile, so I enjoy observing little home-made traditions, like going cod fishing off Dungeness beach on Christmas Eve. I have just decided that I'll tie my opening night to 12 August – and the start of my lamping season. The grouse-shooter's 'glorious' day.

You don't find gardeners digging up seedlings, so although I can't resist the occasional day out to get away from my business, I leave the bunnies strictly alone during March and April. This is when you're likely to shoot pregnant or milky does, and although their flesh is most tender at this time, it just isn't fair. When little patches of fur strew the favourite grazing areas bucks are fighting – a sure sign of the breeding season. Does are lining their nests.

If pest eradication is your aim, then March and April are the time to be about it. It makes me cringe to see farmers out lamping at this time of year, destroying the seedlings of my autumn crop. Rabbits may breed rapidly, but only a tiny percentage of the previous year's stock makes it through the winter. Years ago I went out and lamped around a specific warren. I found plenty of rabbits there and killed seventeen. Nearly all were does full with young. The warren brought forth few bunnies that spring, and stayed virtually abandoned for two years.

I suppose that if a rabbit feels young life

Rabbits use their ears like antennae, to compensate for their low-level vision.

swelling inside her, it is natural that she should be trusting, benign and optimistic for their chances in the world. Despite the education of a hard winter, does just sit and blink in the lamplight, reluctant to run. A milky doe is even worse. She has a family down below which is occupying so much of her time that she can only nip out for a short while. She doesn't want to end her teabreak just because the moon is moving at high speed towards her. Does are an unworthy mark.

There's a time just before the clocks go forward in spring when rabbits will be making the most of the evening sunshine, coming out around tea-time and staying out until the cold comes back at darkness. These longer evenings seem to take humans by surprise. After all the months of cold and darkness, most people have got into the habit of ending early their day outdoors. The dog will have been walked by tea-time. It's as though wild creatures realise that, for the first time in six months, they can have part of the day to themselves.

You may be amazed at how the warrens come to life on these long, golden evenings. You'll see over a dozen rabbits sitting, feeding and chasing where you thought there was only a handful of survivors. For them, the grass is tender and growing fast, the buzz of spring is in the air and they have a lovely evening to themselves. Such evenings also provide the hunter with practically unlimited opportunities for a heavy bag. However, the bucks will take some cooking, even if you can tell them apart from pregnant does that still have their winter coat. One easy way, though, is to watch which rabbits perform scent-marking rituals on others. Bucks mark their does this way.

With a freezer still piled high with the fruits of last season's shooting, I see no point in disturbing their well-being. Most countrymen consider the breeding season as a period of truce between shooters and their quarry.

By the end of May, however, all the early babies will be big enough, and often daft enough, to allow some excellent stalking early and late in the day. This continues through all those glorious weeks as summer unfolds over the countryside. Even when the sun is high you'll be able to stalk a few that are out sunning themselves.

To my mind, glorious hot days are better spent fishing, especially if the bass, mackerel and tope are shoaling off Beachy Head. When the tides are wrong or the weather is too breezy for fishing, I love to be alone on the hills, watching the dawn come up, my footprints a dark trail through the dew. At this magic hour I can lurk in the shadows and intercept rabbits as they return from their night's feeding far out in the fields.

The long summer evenings are ideal for stalking rabbits. Quarry is at its most abundant, allowing you to select just the right size for the pot. It seems that the full-grown adults are always the last to come out of a warren. They leave their children to act as scouts, and often their cowardice is justified.

During the early part of the evening, you'll find bunnies feeding within fifty yards of cover. They are then at their most stalkable because, as the shadows lengthen, they will move further and further away, and far out into the fields. Bunnies can cope with foxes much more easily in the open. When pursued, a rabbit travels at high speed, then turns on a sixpence. A dog's or a fox's momentum has to be stopped and turned while the rabbit, having wrong-footed its pursuer, darts into the bushes. That's why you need two dogs during the daytime, with one covering for the sudden turn.

One excellent way of shooting on these summer evenings is to ambush rabbits as they leave their warrens. If there is no convenient cover, you'll have to build a hide on the east side of your warren. The first reason for this is that the sun sets in the west, allowing you to pick out the silhouettes of rabbits against the afterglow of sunset. That depends on the configuration of the ground, of course. If the exciting sport of silhouette shooting isn't available on your patch, a site west of the warren provides better lighting for late evening shooting.

The hide needs to be semi-permanent if rabbits are to accept it, so you may as well site it in the right place. Much depends on the wind, which obligingly comes out of the west for most of the time, but you have to be careful that your scent isn't wafted down holes that form part of the same complex. The rabbits will then be

A discarded tractor tyre makes a good hide for shooting rabbits in a field behind the barn.

able to pin-point you precisely and will slip out by the furthest hole, possibly well out of range. If this happens, you may have to earth in some of the offending holes.

When rabbits leave their warren late in the evening, they don't linger close to cover, especially if they suspect that something is amiss out there. So it helps if you can shoot from a position about forty yards out in the field that they'll be feeding in. This may be made easy by handy clumps of thistles and nettles. Once you're

set up, it's a good idea to lie out in your hide when the rabbits are underground at noon. Put a scattering of stones or other impromptu targets at the ranges you plan to shoot at, and make sure you can hit them fair and square. Things look different in the dusk, so a couple of flints situated as range markers will do wonders for self-confidence.

It is vital to shoot straight because the last thing you must do is show yourself. Check through the scope that the twitching bunny is indeed past caring, but gather it later, even though a fox comes sidling down the fence. Don't frighten him off – he'll only take one, and the memory will be cherished all your life. Other rabbits will be only slightly disturbed by a silenced shot and they'll come back out again within a quarter of an hour. They'll also check out their slain companions, puzzled by their inert behaviour, but not distressed. *Crack!* Another one keels over.

Get into position early, before they come out en masse. If you prefer to spend part of the time stalking, finishing off with an ambush, reflect that once you have disturbed them by getting into position, it will probably be an hour before they start coming back out again. Much depends on how accustomed they are to disturbance.

I live in beautiful countryside, and one of the favourite tourist walks is down the middle of a little valley that leads to a gap in the cliffs. The rabbits here are so used to trippers that, although the bushes are only ten yards from the path, they often don't bother to hop all the way into cover when people walk past.

I walk there in the evening when the bunnies are dotted all over the grass. Within minutes of my passing, they're back out grazing again. How I'd like to take my rifle down there and teach them some fresh facts of life – they already know too much about the other sort.

Lamping

Summer begins to fade as the evenings grow darker. Now is the time to check the lamp and its battery and make sure the rucksack and other items of equipment are ready for the annual crop of bunnies. And I do mean a crop. My shooting partner, Neil, and I stay out on the hills until we're too tired to carry any more back to the car. It is heavy work, but it lays in an abundant supply of top-quality fresh meat for the dog and I to enjoy during the following year.

We go for large numbers, using the rifle and the dog. If they sit still, as early-season bunnies invariably do, they are shot. If they run, the dog is slipped. We come upon bunches of rabbits and often shoot four or five before the others spook. This way we amass totals of anything between thirty and eighty.

If we didn't, a valuable meat supply would be totally wasted. The farmers are plagued by hordes of bunnies that build up during the summer, and they remind me that numbers need thinning. However, these large numbers have their own safety check. Families of well-grown foxes consume plenty of them, and before September comes in the first signs of myxomatosis will be evident. Within three months, this and predation will have reduced their numbers to about a fifth of what they were at the start of the season.

Our harvest includes many that would have died of disease. Additionally, the bag is so slight on still nights or when the moon is up that it's not worth disturbing the rabbits for so small a return. They wise up soon enough. We make fewer than a dozen trips each season, but when we do make the effort, we go about it ruthlessly. Even so, it takes us about three trips before our night shooting techniques and our physical fitness (along with the dog's) are up to scratch.

From then on, we cover many miles in a night, visiting warren after warren, with the rucksack getting heavier all the while. From time to time we pause to lighten the load by paunching the slain, so it is important to make sure the knife isn't left at home. The foxes will have cleared up the remaining parts before morning. One night I worked a valley, returning after every dozen or so kills to dump them in a central spot where I had a fox-proof sack.

The author and Bryn kitted up for a night's lamping on the Downs.

After four hours, with the tally at fifty-three, I decided to call it a night and paunched the whole lot in one place. Not even the smallest trace of the carnage was to be seen next morning.

One of us shoots, the other wears the lamp and rucksack and keeps the dog on his slip. After losing umpteen leads and lengths of string in the night-shadowed tussocks, I now strap one end of the slip to my wrist. The dog brings to hand any bunnies that are hit, but which run

107

Kitted out for a night's shooting – but reflect that this image will terrify ordinary members of the public.

strongly. Often we discover that we're shooting a bit high because he brings back bunnies with pierced ears. Ranges at night are much closer than they appear to be and most misses go over the top.

Go out on a black night with a fair breeze rustling through the grass and creaking among the blackthorn thickets. Park the car in the lane, switch off the lights and let your eyes become accustomed to the blackness. Listen to the patter of drizzle on the roof, promising perfect conditions. The dog knows it, too. He's standing rigid and alert on the back seat, wearing the special collar that I made him, his flanks quivering as waves of excitement pass through him. Open the doors and get set up. Leave the dog to have a run around – he ought to have the first rabbit, anyway, to warm up on.

Now call him. Up he comes, his eyes reflecting white in the lamplight. He stands, awaiting the lead which he sees as a promise of success. Down in the valley lies a large warren, with rabbits well out on the hill now. Start at the top, and work back towards the warren, sweeping the tussocky grass with the lamp. There. Over there you spot the pale form and the orange gleam of an eye. Quick, walk as fast and as silently as you can until you're well within range. Watch the rabbit. Maybe its ears are turned towards you, its nose gently twitching. It's not bothered. Creep a little closer. Careful now. It caught the sound of a dead flower head banging into your shoe. It crouches down, its ears flat on its back, darting its head this way and that, ready to sprint but unsure of where the track home lies.

Gently wobble the lamp from side to side and it'll freeze again. Raise the rifle, centre the cross-hairs, and softly squeeze the trigger. The skull-splitting crack carries sharply through the night as the bunny slumps on its side. At the sound of

the rifle, a second head pops out of the grass close by. *Crack!* Another perfect head-shot. Look up there, a rabbit is coming in towards cover, disturbed from its feeding further out on the hill.

Quickly walk on to intercept it. No, it's not having any of that. It speeds its pace and suddenly the slip-lead hisses as the dog accelerates away, the loose end flying free from the nylon ring in his collar. Through the tall grass they fly, the rabbit invisible, but the dog repeatedly changing direction and racing off again. Suddenly the rabbit appears on a stretch of short grass as if it's flying six inches off the ground. The dog's hard behind. In the lamplight they both appear as bright airborne shapes against the black night. Then the rabbit halts and races back up the hill again, but the dog read his thoughts and has already slowed. It is a familiar trick.

Back into the tussocks they fly, the dog almost catching a flying heel. The changes are coming faster now, the rabbit realising it has nowhere left to go and scant strength to get there. From the edge of the lamplight comes a squeal, then nothing. A few moments later back he comes, trotting towards us, pausing to rearrange the limp burden in his mouth.

He places it at my feet, but, now that he's so fit that he doesn't need to pant for air, he keeps a firm hold across the shoulders until I take hold. The bunny isn't dead, just shocked and lying doggo, ready to sprint off again as soon as the opportunity presents itself.

A sturdy rabbiting lurcher (mine's a collie/whippet) is invaluable for gathering wounded rabbits. Thankfully, if the dog were to rely on this for his sport, he wouldn't even get warm on some nights. But as a sport in its own right, dogging has to be the fairest. Either the chase ends with a squeal and a kill, or a frustrated bark after quite some workout.

Some nights I add to the freezer by going out on the stubble fields with just my rifle and rucksack. Some of the fields will have been ploughed by mid-October and many warrens will suddenly find themselves on short rations. However, a couple of hedges away lies one of last summer's wheat fields. Maybe you'll find one with banks along two sides, both full of burrows like this.

For the biggest haul ever, you want a period around the full moon when the rabbits know they can go way out and see anything coming for miles. When a cold front rolls in from the west, blotting out all but the occasional pale patch of sky, the bunnies won't think to change their habits. The burrows will stay empty for hours, giving a good opportunity to run out a long net, perhaps.

After weeks of autumn rain, the stubble is soft and barely crackles as you walk down the lanes of crushed stalks where the harvester's tyres trod. The patches of green, where spilled grain has sprouted, are long and sweet, although the bunnies eat the old stalks too. They feel safe in the shaggy cover, believing that they have only to crouch to disappear from view. They do too, so mark each kill carefully. Gather it swiftly if it's winged, or else it'll vanish. This game is about precision killing. Go to a big stubble field on the right night and you could find hundreds of bunnies. Work through it in sweeps across the wind so that your scent is always being blown away from them. Don't be too tempted by bunnies scampering away into the middle of the field – plenty of others are already out there, and you'll have abundant opportunities when you work back again.

I would advise you against what my mate and I once did. We were working a field under perfect conditions. It was about a quarter-mile square, with warrens in the middle and around three sides. The rabbits seemed convinced that the lamp was the moon coming from behind the dense cloud. We bagged eighty, although we left three diseased ones for the foxes. The dog caught at least thirty on his own and brought the winged ones in, too. Neil and I took it in turns to shoot. Once a couple of dozen paunched bunnies were in the rucksack, off one of us would stagger to the car and empty it into the boot. It was all great fun, and the fleas hopping around inside the car reminded us of it for a fortnight.

We should have gone for the ton but we lost count around forty-five and finished when we could barely walk another step. Only fit men should try this sort of sport because the lamp man, who also has the rucksack, often has to sprint uphill after the dog with 50lb of bunnies on his back so as to keep the spotlight hitting the rabbit at full beam. I find it much more fun than blasting bunnies with a twelve-bore out of a Landrover.

Every now and then I read articles which advise lampers to put a red or a blue filter gel over their spotlight. This is because bunnies' eyes are supposed to be less sensitive to blue or red light. That may be so, but a gel reduces light output by at least seventy-five per cent. This in itself is a benefit for those people who suffer from the 'gotta-buy-the-most-powerful' syndrome; as for the rabbits, they couldn't care two hoots what colour the light is, they see it and run without preference.

Sometimes while out quietly lamping, we come across families of foxes stalking groups of bunnies. Generally they'll be far out in a field, or around the end of a rabbit fence. Tactics differ slightly from place to place, but the layout is roughly the same. The foxes are divided into two groups, each on opposite sides of the wind. The majority will be lying flat out within inches of the runs that the rabbits will take

Smack!

as they head for home.

This is what the other one or two foxes are there for. They slowly herd the rabbits towards those in wait, then charge. A brace may fall to this trick – food for the family for a night. Although open hill ambushes vary from place to place, the foxes seem usually to choose to wait

where rabbit fences end. If the bunnies are a doddle for my dog to catch, after driving them into the long grass along the bottom, I doubt if the foxes often fail.

I remember one bunny that was feeding in a field beside the road. I didn't know the ground too well; I was being shown it that night by the farmer, who also was

111

anxious to see what the dog thought of his sheep. I feared lest a chase crossed the road, so I didn't slip the dog. The rabbit still spooked though, dashed into the tussocks beside the field and was neatly fielded by a fox. It was a super catch. The fox, which was lurking downwind, knew that the bunny would probably take the same route home as it had travelled out on, and his guess was spot on.

On an evening of drizzly weather, I was out lamping in a stubble field when I came across a badger. Whole families of these are common out on the stubbles after rain. They go snouting for worms. Well, I shot several rabbits within about a hundred yards of Mr Brock, but he batted not an eyelid. He couldn't smell me, and that's what matters most to badgers. When I got near him, I lamped him and he turned and trotted towards me. I was carrying a fresh-shot rabbit at the time and went to throw it in the tyre-track he was trundling down. But it landed only a few feet away.

He came so close I could see the little grains of sand on his nose where he'd been snouting. He scented the rabbit and came forward slowly, rigidly. Poker-stiff, he smelled it from one end to the other then, relaxing, grabbed it behind the head and trundled off into the bushes, the bunny slung alongside, dragging its heels.

At other times we come across woodcocks and partridges, hares and all sorts out enjoying the night. These we leave well alone. However, often a glint of white in a thorn bush or an ivy tree tells of a roosting magpie, and these villains are fair game any time. So are woodpigeons, although they tend to burst off into the night well before the lamp comes near. Sometimes they'll linger long enough, especially early in the autumn, and you can have good roost shooting like this before they wise up.

Weather

Bunnies are very sensitive to the weather. You have probably heard the old saying 'like rabbits after rain' but that's only the start of it, and then it depends on the time of year. Rabbits act just the same before rain. If you see lots of them out from their warrens early in the evening, there's every chance that a storm will come up before midnight. They sense its approach and feed around it.

They don't like getting wet or cold. This doesn't mean that you won't find them out even in heavy rain, especially at night. Because they feed hunched down in the grass, they come to hand so dry you think they must only just have come out. Once when I was out lamping, the bunnies and I were caught out by such a deluge as I have experienced only in the tropics. The hill soon became a sheet of water as I squelched back towards the car, my backpack and a spare sack both full.

As I bent my back against my load and the rain, I passed within feet of groups of rabbits that were caught out too. They didn't move, even when I walked up close with the lamp. I let them be because I'd run out of ammunition and had too many to carry as it was. But I reckon that the rain had washed out the scent trails that end up at their warrens and they didn't know which way to turn.

Rabbits aren't too keen on frost, either. In hard weather you'll find them making the most of any pale winter sunshine, keeping close to the edge of cover. Sometimes they're hard to spot until they dash away, warning others of your intrusion. If a severe frost threatens, they will come out early in the evening before it gets too cold. But if a front of warmer weather is likely to make the temperature rise later on, they may not come out until well past midnight.

Much depends on your own observa-

112

tions of the bunnies around your shoot. Their habits and routines can vary to a surprising degree. A friend lets me shoot over his farm. There are lots of rabbits, and plenty of banks and tangled undergrowth for them to shelter in. Go there on a summer's evening and you'll see them frolicking everywhere and you'll bag plenty. Try the same trick the next morning at dawn and you'll think it was all a figment of your imagination. You'll be lucky to see a brace.

Myxomatosis

Myxomatosis is less of a scourge nowadays than it used to be. I well remember the outbreak when it first arrived in Britain. Rabbits were to be seen dead and dying all around the field in front of the house. It was a ghastly time. Perhaps ninety-nine per cent of an enormous, stable population was wiped out. Many warrens have never been repopulated in some parts of the world. However, a virus with such a strong impact is likely to wipe itself out. The strain we have now is much weaker, and rabbits are gradually building an immunity to it.

The disease originates from South America. There, they have built a strong immunity to the disease, the only sign of infection is a slight swelling at the base of each ear. In Britain you are likely to come across bunnies with slight swellings, like skin tumours, but few other symptoms. They may be a bit mucky around the eyes, but nothing serious. A few weeks later you'll be shooting rabbits with bright eyes and signs where the skin lesions have healed, although the fur has yet to grow back.

The disease is spread by fleas. Because these lovable fellows are so tiny, their stomach readily becomes blocked by bacteria, be it myxomatosis or bubonic plague.

Starving hungry, they indulge in a frenzy of biting, sometimes regurgitating the virus into the bites along with the blood they can't swallow. They're also capable of transmitting mange and tapeworms. Pretty dynamic fleas!

I really felt cheated during my teens by the devastation left behind by myxomatosis. Perhaps this book is the consequence of a subconscious desire to make good the deficit, at a time of life when most people are losing sleep over their careers, office politics, and the kids' schooling.

But rabbits are tough little critters and it didn't take them long to make a comeback. They're almost as numerous as they used to be in many parts of the country. There's every chance, if nobody plays tricks with the myxomatosis virus, that they'll ultimately build full resistance before the turn of the century.

I don't think this has anything to do with rabbits spending more time living above ground. I've never seen any evidence to support this theory. They love to lie out in remote bramble bushes and thistle clumps, knowing they can give the dog a hard chase, stitch him up, and dive down a burrow.

Rabbits are difficult to hit, too. It's best if you clout them in the head, but even then you'll be amazed when they get up and run twenty-five yards before dropping stone-dead. Look at what the pellet did to its skull, and you'll understand why shooters tell you that a dead rabbit can run. Heart and neck shots are fine if you're close enough. Don't fire into the body – ever. If the rabbit has its back to you, click your tongue or whistle to make it sit up, but have the rifle ready on aim in case it sees you move, and bolts. If it won't sit up, wait until its head is raised or to one side. This requires precision to avoid a wounding body shot.

With a kill area of half an inch showing, but a woundable area of half a foot, often it is better not to take a shot like this.

Paunching, Skinning and Cooking

You'll need that sharp knife when you come to paunch rabbits. The trick is to lay the rabbit on its back and stick the point into the body cavity between the back legs. Hold the knife at a shallow angle, blade outwards, and slip it quickly between the skin and intestines as far as the rib-cage. With the rabbit on its back, you'll have no trouble steering the point just under the belly skin. This prevents the knife, only an inch of which is inside the bunny, from rupturing the intestines and causing an appalling, smelly mess. (This is the best reason I know for never stopping for run-over rabbits, especially after the pressure has injected all last week's dinners deep into the flesh).

Now open the cavity and with the fingers of your right hand find the liver and hold it in place. The left fingers separate the stomach from the body with a gentle pull, but don't actually remove it. Now, with the rabbit still on its back, take the front paws in your right hand and the back paws in your left hand and turn the bunny on to its left side, the paunch opening facing you. Now swing the rabbit off the ground and out to the right. When you feel the power coming on, flick your left hand and simultaneously let go with your right hand. The entire intestine

will fly out cleanly. Once you've mastered this simple, moderately hygenic trick, it's the quickest most tasteful means of paunching there is.

I paunch every bunny I shoot in the field, and thread the back legs so that they can cool in the garage. The next morning – particularly in the hot, early part of the season – I set to skinning them. Faced by a pile of bunnies, I take a block and chopper and remove heads and paws. Then the skin is peeled around the back from the body cavity and, holding the body in one hand, the skin in the other, it's pulled first from the hind part, then off from the neck. Big bucks are tough to skin, but it

Presented like this, a rabbit's kill area is extensive.

doesn't take long to get the knack, provided you pull hard.

Now bend the tail, grip it hard and twist away both tail and anus. Stick a little finger inside the cavity to push clear any remaining intestine and the bladder. Remove the testicles from a buck. The area between the legs should be clear, else dishes cooked later will be tainted. Finally, remove the gall-bladder from the liver. A hard, pale or white-blotched liver is a sign of an unhealthy rabbit. A dark purple liver makes a delicious pâté particularly with sherry. And as for the kidneys, remove them all and fry them with bacon for breakfast – stunning.

Bunnies taste best after long, slow cooking. My dog and I have refined the technique. With three in a stewing pot with a couple of inches of water, they get an hour at 150°C and another two hours at 100°; sometimes even longer at less. Once they're done, the meat breaks cleanly from the bone, without any trace of rubberiness. The dog has his straight from the pot, without trimmings. But get a mass of best bacon, plenty of onions, carrots, potatoes and herbs, cook them with the rabbit pieces and you'll have a first-class stew. Bon appetit.

9 Squirrels, Rats and Mustelids

This chapter includes details of hunting for the grey squirrel, brown rat and, if predator control requires, mink, stoat and weasel. There are also three protected species in these family groups: the red squirrel, black rat and the pine marten. If any of these are known to visit your shoot, make sure you can differentiate them from legitimate quarry.

Squirrels

One of my favourites is the grey squirrel. It's a handsome and tricky quarry – rarely as easy to hit as you hope, but often giving opportunities that really bring out the marksman in you. I can think of several very satisfying shots I've had at squirrels. One day I was so much on form that it seemed as though a supernatural force was steering my shots. I think I was feeling super-fit, or something, but the cross-hairs seemed to sit untrembling on every mark I went for. It was great. I came across a squirrel at extreme range. I was standing in a valley, and the little animal was sitting at the top of a tall larch growing out of the bank. The squirrel was out on a branch, its silvery tail looped like a handle on its back, about a foot away from the trunk. It was a long, high shot. To make it harder, a thin tracery of larch twigs hung between us.

Mounting the rifle, I found my mark. The squirrel was watching me, but through the six-power scope I could also see twigs that would interfere with my shot. Some, almost out of focus, were close to me. Others were right in front of my mark. I carefully shuffled to one side, keeping the squirrel in the sights until I could see clear sky all the way through. I aimed high, well aware that my pellet would have to pass half an inch under one twig if it was to find its mark and not ricochet harmlessly into the tree. With the cross-hairs about two inches above its eye, and without a sign of a tremble, I softly squeezed the trigger. The squirrel leapt from its branch, and sailed through the air, tumbling down the bank and landing stone-dead at my feet in a patter of autumn leaves. I'd hit exactly where I'd intended.

I have pulled off some memorable shots at moving targets. They're easy to miss by miles. If you're presented with a squirrel racing through the trees swing past its nose, keep the cross-hairs there, and when the moment looks right, push through a bit faster and squeeze at about six inches past its whiskers, keeping swinging. Naturally, your own technique may differ from mine, but this is the way I learned to shoot moving targets. The difference between shooting this way and with a shot-gun is that you have first to find a precise sight picture with a rifle. Running squirrels rarely offer such an opportunity. Shot-gun shooters use a tubeful of shot which they swing like an extension of their right arm. All those dozens of pellets permit much greater fluency of action.

Squirrels have preferred feeding places, and marked routes from these to their dreys. Some of these highways pass over long branches which act as bridges between one mass of cover and another. It is on these that you can take moving shots as the squirrel scampers across in front of you. Be quick and decisive or your mark will be gone. Get it right, though, and the squirrel will be knocked flying off the branch. As you pick it up and see the tell-tale bead of blood staining the fur above its heart, you'll think to yourself 'Did I do that?'

Squirrels aren't popular with foresters because they have a passion for nibbling at growing shoots. This can result in mis-shapen mature trees, thus lowering the ultimate size and value of the crop. I feel moved to remark that humans are incredibly arrogant to condemn a wild creature simply because its mode of life clashes with the presumed needs of man. Nevertheless, foresters have quite a strong case because the grey is not only an introduced species, but it has ousted the smaller red squirrel from much of its natural habitat. The reason I hunt squirrels is because the estate I shoot on has been given over almost entirely to wildlife projects. Grey squirrels are curious animals and like to meddle wherever they can. They also have a taste for the pupae of one of Britain's rarest butterflies, the purple emperor.

The grey is quite capable of holding its own: though like all wild creatures, the young are incredibly naïve early in the autumn. You'll find it necessary to wear full camouflage for squirrel shooting. They have very sharp eyes and often slip away before you're in range. At times they will sit frozen on a branch as you walk past. You, too, need sharp eyes to pick them out from the leaves and branches.

Very often you'll see them chasing each other through the boughs, allowing you to plan a stalk. Yet from their high vantage point they can spot every movement beneath them, and often there just isn't enough cover to allow you to get within range.

Much depends on how jumpy your squirrels are. Because of all the conservation projects on the estate, the squirrels get hammered by my friend and his twelve-bore. Nowadays they race away to the thickest yew tree or belt of conifers like scalded cats. If squirrels don't feel as persecuted as this, they'll often run to a tree, climb up about five yards, then clamp to the trunk or a branch, if there isn't a hole or a drey to shelter in. As you walk around the trunk, you'll catch the sight of fur, then as you creep into position for a shot, the squirrel will sidle further around the trunk, probably climbing even higher.

The trick is to place your coat or something highly visible on the ground a few yards away from the side of the tree you started from and hope that as you and the squirrel play hide-and-seek around the trunk, it'll decide that the coat is more threatening than you, allowing you to get it into your sights. However, it doesn't often work like this, and you'll be presented with plenty of opportunities for vertical snap shooting. Remember that when you're shooting vertically, the pull of gravity on the pellet is at right angles to how it was when you zeroed the rifle, so the trajectory is completely different. Aim slightly low. Better still, take a few vertical shots at the undersides of dead branches and mark how the point of impact differs from your point of zero.

Squirrels spend a lot of time in their dreys. These are untidy clumps of leaves and branches in the cleft of a tree or woven into the ivy. An old drey is a thin, skimpy affair, with many of its leaves blown away by winds. Those that are in use look new, with plenty of fresh leaves woven into the structure.

On occasions, I have chased squirrels out of their dreys. With so much thick thatch around them, it sometimes takes four or five shots before the occupants come scampering out on to the branches or go racing away through the trees in search of a safer hole. Often their reaction is to dive out of the drey, run up the trunk

a few feet and clamp themselves to the trunk while they check out the situation. Reload slowly or you'll be spotted and it'll be back to games of hide-and-seek around the trunk with lots of twigs to steer a telling shot through.

I have now decided that it isn't fair to shoot at dreys. It is possible to kill a squirrel in its bed, but the chances are higher that a wounded animal will emerge. As it is the hunter's duty to avoid

A trio of grey squirrels is the reward for a snowy afternoon in the woods.

this at all costs, I prefer to let them slumber undisturbed, biding my time for when the weather is right.

Squirrels like cheerful weather. They hibernate for parts of the winter, but strong sun in even the thickest snow will bring out some to scratch around for their buried stores of nuts. The best of the shooting has to be in the autumn woods after the first storms have thinned the leaves a bit. Go out on a fine, sunny morning and you'll never find the woods more enchanting.

I love to see the changing autumn colours, along with all the signs of game. These are abundant after the breeding season. Squirrels are everywhere, too, and in the sunshine they'll be foraging all over the forest floor and high in their favourite trees. There's no need to chase them out of bed on a morning like this. By mid-afternoon you should have quite a mixed bag – with squirrels, pigeons and maybe a magpie or jay – after walking and stalking for several miles through magnificent scenery. You'll probably end up far from home and feeling ravenously hungry, especially if there's a nip of frost in the air.

Perhaps I should have a more serious mind, but I have to confess that one of the greatest attractions that hunting holds for me is that it allows me to enjoy my hobby amid lovely scenery and beautiful countryside. Then, when I do get home, there's absolutely no doubt that I'll do full justice to all those delicious smells that are wafting from the kitchen. Maybe they'll be from the produce of other hunts.

There's an important point that has to be observed if you're going to shoot well in woodland – you've got to hide your face, even if that means painting it with blobs of camouflage make-up. Very often you will have to move about with your face pointing skywards, searching for either the quarry or a useful sight picture.

But wild creatures feel uncomfortable when they see that little pink moon shining up at them. By hiding it, you'll be less likely to spook your quarry, giving you longer to compose your sight picture before squeezing off a shot.

Rats

I don't think that rats are very lovable, even though people keep them as pets. Mind you, these are nicely sanitised creatures compared to the wild brown rat. This little fellow is linked to some of man's greatest moments of squalor, like the Black Death and the trenches during World War One. Outbreaks of bubonic plague are now rare, but rats still carry diseases, like tetanus and Weil's syndrome, both of which can kill. Obviously you don't mess with rats, but if one bites you see your doctor straight away.

It is these undesirable aspects that make people dislike rats so much. Even though they're clean little animals, the diseases they carry are about as appalling as the filthy places where they live – sewers, rubbish dumps, and neglected areas. During the summer, rats spend quite a lot of time in the fields, often in colonies along the banks of ditches. Then they aren't easy to shoot because the cover is generally too long, although a bit of pruning will improve your chances of a clear shot. You should remember that rats are fair game to cats, owls, and foxes. This is quite enough reason for them to be very shy at times.

Once the cover goes, many rats make tracks to farm buildings and similar sheltered areas where they can spend the winter in dry, comfortable conditions, with plenty of food close by. This migration starts soon after harvest time, especially if heavy rains come early. You'll notice the occasional specimen that has been

Ambushing rats in the farmyard from atop a pile of pallets.

flattened on the road.

You don't have to wait until this late in the year to get to grips with rats, lots of them linger around farm buildings throughout the year. It is here that they do most damage, especially to sackfuls of feed and seed, and most farmers would prefer to be without them.

Whether or not you'll be allowed to shoot around the farmyard is something else again. Some farmers may have visions of you blinding the cowman, causing hugely expensive claims for damages. A lot depends on the farm, though. Modern farm buildings and yards consist of areas of solid concrete. This denies rats the cluttered corners and overgrown ditch banks where they build up stable warrens. However, there are still plenty of scruffy, old-fashioned farms around.

When shooting rats around farm buildings, you probably won't want a powerful rifle because of the danger of ricochets in a confined space. This applies particularly when shooting inside barns. Rats live among the rafters as much as under the walls, so frequently you will be presented with opportunities to swat them out of the roof. If the gun is too powerful, you could end up smashing tiles. Even worse, you may break a window. If broken glass falls among hay for feed, you'll have to explain it to an angry farmer.

First, you have to find your stock of rats. Look for their runs, holes, droppings, and for signs of foraging. The classic case of the nibbled sack, with corn running out of the hole, is only too familiar to farmers everywhere. Indeed, these animals are so indiscreet that they readily give away their presence.

You have to study them, though, just like any other wild animal, if you're to have worthwhile shooting instead of a long, lonely wait. They're pretty active by day and by night. It all depends on the amount of disturbance they are subjected to, so obviously this has to be borne in mind. However, rats become most active once the sun has set.

Get up on the bales of sweet-scented hay and wait for the action. Settle yourself comfortably, for under these conditions you can ensure maximum steadiness by shooting from the field target competitor's sitting position, or by using a bale as a rest. Below you, in the pens, calves are settling for the night, and the piglets have gone into a huddle in a straw-filled corner. Apart from the occasional contented grunt or soft rustling, all is quiet.

A lone bulb hangs low from the rafters of this ancient, flint barn. At its opposite end, just twenty yards away, the feed milling machine lies silent in the cold glare of the lamp. Beside it stands a wide, stone-walled bay. It's piled with barley – and rat droppings.

And there's the first. Keeping close to the wall, a dark shape comes sidling out of the darkened corner, heading for the bay. Through the scope you can see it scuttling a few feet, then stopping to case the joint, its bright eyes and twitching whiskers reaching out for signs of danger. Centre the cross-hairs just below the ear and a little in front. Quick now, before it makes the shelter of the milling machine, take it at the next pause. There. It stops, and up

comes its snout, testing the air as you touch the trigger. The shot snatches it with a loud plop, flinging it against the crumbling flint wall. The back legs twitch a couple of times, but it's all over.

Moments later, a movement from on top of the wall beside the bay catches your eye. There's another one, sitting on the edge of the shadows in the corner, hunched up and watching, its scaly tail drooping over the side of the wall. Through the scope you see not one, but two rats, one partly hidden by the other, and it looks like the front one is staring straight at you. Disconcerting though it is, it's just coincidence. There's no way the big old critter could detect you. Centre the cross-hairs between its eyes and squeeze before it shuffles away. With a reflex leap it jumps into the bay and sprawls amid the barley. At the same time there's a terrified shriek as the other rat races along the wall and dives for one of the emergency exits.

Don't break cover, though. Ten minutes later, another rat comes out, this time from the same corner as the first one. Seeing the first corpse, it stops and goes to investigate. It seems to be sniffing it most intently. Through the scope you observe just how repulsive rats really are – this one is lapping the blood of its fallen comrade – much more nourishing than barley. Keep a steady bead and make sure it catches the next shuttle to the great sewer in the sky.

A friend in Wales has an excellent way of shooting rats. He puts out a slab of rock on the edge of a stream along which the rats go about their nightly business. He baits the rock. One night he goes with a lamp and throws a soft beam on to the rock. A rat jumps on to the rock, grabs a piece of food, and jumps off again into the overhanging grass. The next one is much slower and pays the price. Five minutes later another appears. It's a good sport for two people on a winter's evening, and bags of a couple of dozen or more are common. It trains you to shoot quickly. You can set up the same type of baited trap in deserted buildings, rubbish tips and other rat havens.

Mustelids

Occasionally a stoat, weasel or mink makes its presence felt. The first two provoke the anger of gamekeepers everywhere by destroying the nests of gamebirds – so do squirrels, incidentally. Although mink destroy nests and kill birds, because they prefer to live close to water their main enemies are fishery managers. They behave rather like otters and have the bad habit of only eating a couple of bites from a fish before diving for the next one. Like us, they're predatory sportsmen.

When a mink gets into a trout farm, it finds itself presented with opportunities beyond the limits of its imagination. A pair of mink, coursing trout like a pair of greyhounds, will have a great time and cause hundreds of pounds worth of damage. This is why permanent cage traps lie alongside every ditch and stream leading into and out of these farms.

I'm reluctant to shoot them, even though mink are numerous enough in some places to require culling. They're partial to eggs and nestlings, so you won't see many songbirds where mink are common. They're efficient little hunters, like the rest of their family. It's an instinct the species appears not to have lost during the years in captivity after some were first imported. This is where they came from – specimens that escaped from farms and set up home in the wild. Mink come in all colours, but they seem to revert to dark brown in the wild.

Maybe one instinct has been lost, however, and that's fear. Mink are generally pretty casual about humans, you can get

within yards of one. It'll dart its head out from behind tussocks or from holes in the bank, checking up on you, but not running.

The problem with any of this crew is hitting them. Their main characteristic is hyperactivity, which doesn't allow you much space to squeeze in an effective shot. You'll always have to take your chances as they present themselves, because most of the time one of these critters will suddenly be there in front of you. If you must shoot, now's the time, before it realises what you are and runs off. Slowly lift the rifle. This gentle movement may quite possibly hold its attention, but don't be too long in finding your mark and shooting.

Another method is to stake out a bait. It's the same trick that works for crows and magpies, except that the location is changed to stoat, weasel or mink country. Much depends on the degree to which you're involved with vermin control, but this strikes me as a tedious way to spend a day in the field.

I prefer to watch this trio on their hunting trips. Every rabbit knows that when a weasel or stoat gets on to its trail, it's as good as finished. The little animals follow the trail of just one chosen bunny until it just sits and squeals in sheer terror, waiting for the end. But nature is kind to bunnies, in its way. As soon as the rabbit feels the touch of the stoat, it'll be half dead through shock, and fading rapidly.

Another reason for not hunting them is that all three are accomplished ratters. In many places they may be doing a great deal of good to the environment by keeping down the rat population. If this is the case, they can hardly be called vermin.

For my part, I find their antics interesting, and frequently most comical. One day when I was out fishing a little river, I watched a young mink working its way in my direction along the opposite bank.

123

When it was almost level with me, it dived into the water and nosed around at the bottom of a stand of reeds. It emerged a few minutes later with an eel between its jaws. The eel wasn't very big, but it had no intention of being dragged out of the river and eaten. It lashed and thrashed around, squirming around the mink like a boa constrictor, with the little animal snapping and biting at it all the time. Eventually the mink found the right part, and the eel fell limp. It was dragged under a clump of dock leaves from which my ears caught the occasional sound of scrunching.

10 Woodpigeons and Doves

There are many people in the shooting world, people whose opinions are highly regarded, who consider the woodpigeon to be the best gamebird of the lot. The reason is the variety of shots that woodies present. They can come into roost or scatter around the decoys from practically any direction. A friend, who admits to being an absolute nut about decoying them, has won several national and international championships at skeet and sporting clays.

It's not just the variety and exacting nature of the shooting that appeals, either. Woodies can be shot in a variety of situations, each one requiring the careful application of method and field craft before success is achieved. The hunter has to overcome a wariness in woodies that is legendary, even though they're not as sharp-witted as magpies and crows. This wariness has been instilled by centuries of appealing too much to the human palate.

These characteristics make the woodie a favourite with air rifle hunters, too. It's impossible to take flying shots with any degree of certainty, and because the bird is armour-plated with feathers, this shouldn't be attempted. However, every other form of pigeon shooting that is enjoyed by the shot-gun shooter can also be enjoyed by the rifle man. Bags won't be so big because of the inability to shoot flying birds, but under some circumstances, the air rifle increases the bag through its quietness. I've shot woodies from a hide while they have been coming in to roost. After each shot, they'd fly off, circle round and land again. A few decoys encouraged this obliging behaviour. When I took a friend there with his shotgun a couple of nights later, he had one shot and missed. The flock decamped to a wood two miles up the valley.

Woodies are gradually learning not to hang around when the shooting starts. When they're feeding on rape, which is now grown in great abundance for its oil, woodies have so much choice that a shotgun shooter may get just one shot, even with a perfect decoy pattern. This makes the entire army of woodies take to the air and disappear. You can just make out the dwindling line of dots as they cross the county boundary.

Where to find Woodpigeons

Woodpigeons are fair game all through the year, although I don't like to shoot too heavily during the breeding season. At other times of the year, the air rifle hunter may as well take every opportunity he can. There are, after all, plenty of times when the first indication of one is an explosive clatter from the trees.

During the hard weather of winter, soon after the year has turned, most of their favourite foods are unavailable and they have to make the best of what's about. Sometimes the only things available are kale or Brussels sprouts poking through the snow. A field like this may attract large flocks of pigeons, especially if the snow has wiped out everything else for miles. At such times, pigeons ruin crops intended for humans or their livestock. The damage they can do to a field of greenstuff is legendary.

No farmers tolerate their presence, but they may be reluctant to stay out in the snow, even to save their crop. They'd much rather that you or I came up with the idea of setting up a hide with a few decoys, and gave the birds a pasting. It's a bit unfair, though, because most of them will be thin and wasted by the harsh weather. Disease hits them hard at this time. Often the cold makes them so desperate for food that they become almost tame. Such shooting could hardly be considered difficult, satisfying (unless they're on your sprouts), or sporting.

Up in the woods, late January is when the ivy thinks it's the right time of year to bear fruit. These hard little green berries don't compare to half-ripe grains of wheat, but the woodies have to be thankful to stay alive. You can arrange for this to be otherwise by setting up a hide close to the tree which is most prolific in bearing fruit, and therefore is attracting the most

The woodpigeon – ideal game for the air rifle.

Plastic decoy woodpigeons.

attention. This situation may not last more than a few days, especially if a lot of birds are working it. Sport with an air rifle is fast and excellent when the woodies are going well on the ivy trees. If you wish, set up a couple of flappers like woodies trying to keep their balance on the slender ivy branches. Use lofting poles, hiding them inside the ivy's foliage.

The decoys bring pigeons into your marked tree. But because woodies tend to switch allegiances for no particular reason, you may find that a different tree begins to exercise a pull. I've had some thrilling stalks amid woodland and shelter belts after woodies that have played this trick on me. After an hour of having nothing near me, I've decided to take the risk of falling between two stools, as the saying goes. Sometimes I've been spotted. The secret of getting it right is to keep them all under observation and to go as flat as possible from stump to bush until you're in range.

Mark how many birds are in the tree, and when they're all engrossed in feeding, stealthily move forward to the next bit of cover. Pause a while before peeping round it, though, in case your movement was spotted. Now assess the situation

Take care with pigeons above you – the pellet will fly high unless you aim low.

again. One is staring in your direction. Withdraw your head gingerly and wait a while. Another slow peep. All's well. Crawl forward on elbows and toes to the clump of hazel. You can shoot from there. Just before you reach it there's a frantic clattering of wings. Oh, no! You haven't spooked them, have you? No, it was just a couple of birds both falling off their twigs while going for the same bunch of berries.

They settle again, the one on a dead branch, the other on the ivy behind the tree. Take slow, careful aim at the bird on the branch. He's not looking like going anywhere right now. Probably a bit peeved

about being knocked off his perch by that other greedy fellow. Gently now, creep to one knee and poke the rifle through the hazel stems, crouching as low as possible. Set the scope just below the elbow of its wing and squeeze off. Comes a loud thock, through the frozen winter wood. The woodie slumps down on its toes and slowly tumbles forward, stone dead before it leaves its branch.

After one such stalk, I reached my chosen firing point to find that the half-dozen pigeons in the tree had all vanished. I was just about to start craning my neck to make sure, when a rustle caught my attention. The birds had settled on the grass between myself and the ivy tree. They were pecking at that for a change. I would have spooked them for sure if I hadn't caught that sound of a dead leaf being rustled. As it was, my firing position was a cave of ivy. In the late afternoon light, the cave was full of shadows. I adjusted my position and took aim on the first bird, about fifteen yards away. It collapsed at my shot. Some of the others fled at the sound, but one lingered. The shot pigeon didn't even stir, which must have given the other one confidence. Cautiously I reloaded the rifle, took careful aim, and made it a brace.

As the year starts to warm up, roost shooting comes into its own. Woodies have preferred roosts which they use time after time, especially if the place isn't subject to bad weather. A hill with a crown of trees is always favourite because one side or t'other is warmer, depending on the strength and direction of the wind.

So much varies from wood to wood. For example, woodies often sit out among open trees before tucking up in the heart of a conifer. At other times they'll pitch straight into their beds and will hardly budge, except to flutter from one branch maybe to a lower one. As the hunter on your own patch, it's up to you to work out how to make best use of the opportunities that come your way. Winter roosts are usually quite different from those that are favoured during the summer and autumn. Even so, the woodies give their presence away not just by being around as the sun starts dipping over the edge of the world, but by the greeny-white droppings that form piles and intricate patterns on the woodland floor.

A handful of decoys always helps pigeons to make up their minds about where to bed down for the night. So if you want a full session, it pays to use decoys. Without them, incoming birds see empty trees below them in a place where, and at

a time when, they expect to see plenty of activity. If the wood is empty and pigeonless, all but the dimmest will fly right on over rather than turn back into the wind, their wings set, to glide into the ash tree above your head.

As with other forms of upward-shooting, make sure you camouflage your face, especially where you have to peer through twigs to get a clear shot at your quarry. Woodies know all about little patches of pink dodging through the undergrowth and they won't pause long enough to find out whether you're a hunter or St Francis of Assisi.

Only by watching is it possible to know where to ambush woodies – whether it's at their roosts or their feeding grounds. If you find their favourite diner, you'll have great sport. All you have to remember is that woodies like their food to be plentiful, readily available without scratching, and of the highest gastronomic quality. Woodies are content only with the good things in life.

Later in the season, you'll find them out where the farmers are drilling the new year's crops. Barley is a favourite, but peas and a variety of different seeds bring them flocking. Drilling time spells an end to all those months on a diet of harsh greenery. All those little pellets of protein are just what they need, and it seems they can spot a part-drilled field from five miles away or more.

For best sport, find out from the farmer which day he plans to sow seed. Because woodies can't scratch for food, they can only glean the seeds that lie on the surface after the tractor has passed. It doesn't take a big flock very long to clean out a field, so they're always quick to arrive as soon as they notice the soil changing colour as it is being worked. If other farmers are out drilling, the chances are that plenty of flocks will be around. And the more pigeons there are, the sooner they'll clean the fields and have to look elsewhere.

Set up your hide where you judge the woodies will arrive. It may be a big, dead tree in a hedge, or a small group of oaks. By walking around with a pair of binoculars, but without a gun, you come to notice which trees the woodies like to sit in. Major Archie Coates, the doyen of decoying, coined the phrase 'sitty trees'. It is a valuable term, because it describes the sort of trees that woodies regularly frequent. As a general rule, they're somewhat bare and stand a bit apart, commanding a good view of the landscape.

You can either shoot the woodies as they arrive to case the field, or you can take them when they settle to feed. Obviously that's what they have come for. You'll be amazed at how some start pecking almost before they have folded their wings. The decoy pattern has so convinced them that they can't wait to stuff their crop. The situation couldn't be better. If you can, get a few handfuls of seed off the farmer before you start, a sprinkling in the right place will keep the birds occupied until you are ready to shoot. They may not notice the frozen stance of the birds around them.

Once you have bagged a few, set them up too, by pegging their heads high with sticks. The more you build up your decoy

A dead woodpigeon pegged out as a decoy.

pattern, the more attractive the woodies will find it. If they're coming thick and fast, you'll have trouble keeping them away – especially if you use a silenced air rifle. If you shoot accurately and score heart, neck or head shots on the birds out there, they'll just slump over. Some of the birds will fly at the shot. Often a few linger, sitting bolt upright, blinking their eyes, seeking the danger. But you'll be lucky to get a third shot unless the group that flew away has circled around and come back in again.

Sometimes woodies become suicidal and you'll have a big bag to carry home. At other times, the best laid plans fail abysmally. Maybe the woodies see through your fraud, or maybe they've been taken by the mood to be away somewhere else. These days happen, but they make the great times all the more worthwhile. Nevertheless, you have to be careful when decoying that your birds aren't facing the wrong way after a change in the wind. Every now and then, in lulls in the action, creep out of your hide and set up the slain.

Check that none of the decoys are looking strange, then get rid of any clumps of feathers. If your killing zone is littered with them the birds may shy away. When everything goes to plan, you'll have plenty of opportunities to shoot. Fire through the hide and never poke your face over the top. Every trace of you has to be hidden, but the hide must allow you a wide arc of fire, as you never know where the birds may land.

Spring

As spring gets going the trees come into leaf, and for many woodland hunters this is an excellent time for mooching around the woodies' favourite trees. The extra cover allows you to spot them, with less

chance of them spotting you first. However, it's always tough to stalk woodies. It's all very well to creep up undetected on to one you can see in a far tree. It's those that are sitting unnoticed that give the game away. I have often been surprised at the number of woodies that have burst from trees – maybe twenty where I'd marked just two or three.

It doesn't take long for the leaves to thicken up. In many areas, the only signs of woodies will be sounds of cooing echoing from the canopy above. Sometimes one will fly on to a convenient branch, offering a fair mark; but most times they're inaccessible. There won't be much point in hunting the woods again until autumn thins the foliage. There is one opportunity, though, if plenty of woodies frequent your shoot. Find the areas where they like to take the evening sunlight. There, on warm evenings, they'll flirt and coo around the trees.

Courtship appears to require a great deal of flying around beneath the canopy of leaves. The birds don't stay still for long; but they have favourite branches where they flap about, perhaps as part of the ritual. Find such a place and you'll have a great evening's shooting. You may not need to travel far, either. Large gardens are favourite with woodies, especially if there are plenty of tall trees that the males can chase the females around. Such a place must only be lightly shot if the woodies are to feel confident enough to gather there at roosting time.

Some gardens are excellent places to shoot woodies. I don't just mean pot-shots from the bedroom window, early on a summer's morning, while they're picking at the young clover shoots on the lawn. A relative of mine has a large garden with tall trees around the boundary. The woodies love this. I have decided that the trick to shooting them is to stand in one place and cover two sides from beneath an ornamental weeping cherry tree. It's like being inside a green tent – an excellent natural hide.

Sometimes I'll hear the clatter of wings above my head. I can't cover these tree-tops from my hide, so I have to walk out on to the lawn to take a shot. When I'm about to come into view, I turn round, with the rifle mounted at my shoulder and ready to shoot. Taking a few small paces back on to the lawn, the pigeon's head becomes visible from behind the foliage. As expected, he's sitting on that topmost dead twig. A tiny step more, and the breast and neck come into view. He's seen your movement and is staring straight into the scope, his orange beak and yellow eye giving him a menacing expression. But this woodie believes that anybody in a garden is just strolling around, enjoying the evening air. Besides, he can only see the top of your head and the front of the rifle – not enough to terrify, unless there's too much pink face staring up at him. Take careful aim, work out how the shot will travel, then squeeze off. The problem may come later when you go to retrieve the pigeon. Dense foliage acts like an inverted umbrella and often catches birds falling through it. Great for the blue-bottles and swallows, but not much good for your pigeon pie.

My favourite angle for taking a woodie is with it partly turned sideways on to me, exposing its side for a heart shot. About the worst angle possible is straight into the breast. Not only is this covered by a dense thatch of feathers, but the crop is likely to be stuffed with wadding. At the end of the day, especially when the birds have been gorging themselves on wheat, their crops will be bulging with the stuff. A straight-on shot is likely to result in a severely wounded woodie flying off to a lingering death – bad news. It is always a better policy to hang on for a while.

It's unwise to aim for the centre of the chest – the obvious point – because so much of the bird may be shielded by a crop full of corn.

Maybe ten minutes or more will pass before a settled bird shifts position. But when it does, a sure shot will bag it. If you're impatient, the bird will fly off wounded and the result will be a distasteful failure.

One of the advantages of shooting in gardens is that you never have any problem with range. When deciding on where to hide, you'll have noticed the favourite perches. Before the action starts, take a few practice shots at leaves or fir-cones around where you expect the birds to land. That way, when one drops in at distant range, you'll know for sure how much extra height to give the cross-hairs in order to secure the bird.

A woodpigeon prospects a field of ripening wheat.

Summer

As the cornfields begin to turn gold, the pigeons stuff themselves full of wheat. They like those places where the wind has flattened part of the crop, giving them easy access to the ripening ears. As ever, the fluttering of bluey-white wings from afar is the best guide as to where to set up a hide. This is fairly simple in a cornfield – with plenty of stems to weave into an alcove, there's rarely any problem with the hide not matching the landscape. Because air rifle shooters take their birds sitting, the hide can be a totally unobtrusive cocoon right in the middle of the field, a little back from the edge of the flattened area. With a handful of decoys out, the woodies respond well to so safe-looking an arrangement. They prove to be more willing to be decoyed to the middle of a field rather than the edges, particularly if cover is thick alongside, and is therefore more likely to harbour the likes of you and me.

Autumn

Harvest time is one of my favourite times for shooting pigeons. I know of a copse on a hill overlooking a sea of cornfields. This

133

copse is off-limits to shot-gun shooters because gamebirds are reared there, but my air rifle and I are free to wander through it. That's not the best way to get action though.

The woodies have definite flight lines, both into and out of the wood. These may change by as much as fifty yards according to the wind strength and direction. Nevertheless, it soon becomes apparent which part of the wood is favourite for the day. This is where to set the hide, to take birds as they come in off the stubbles to rest. Not that they always do rest. Often a few will be courting among the tree trunks, and sometimes these birds will perch so close that you'll both be horrified.

The copse that I shoot has a field alongside it which is planted with corn some years. When this is harvested, I site my hide on the edge of the field close by the roosting area. A handful of decoys are ample to bring birds within range. Quite frequently the birds will fly out over the field after my shot, circle around and land in the trees above my head. However, I'm very aware that this situation could be over-exploited. There's no doubt in my mind that the copse is both landing strip and flying club to the woodies. As such it represents the summer headquarters of my local pigeon population, so I limit the amount of harassment they receive from my rifle.

At about this same time of year you can have great sport with woodpigeons at their watering holes. These may be cattle drinks where the water comes almost to the top along one edge. If they fall into one of these drinks, they often can't get out, and drown. That's why the water has to be within easy reach. If the cattle drinks can't provide water, though, they'll visit ponds and pools where they can get down to the water's edge with ease.

One characteristic of a favourite drinking

Woodpigeon – 'a sitting duck'!

site is a good open view. This applies particularly to ponds. Woodies prefer one with firm, gently-shelving sides and not much cover to hide predators. They'll often have a dally and a flirting session around their drinking places, so it pays to find out which are the preferred ones. Fresh feathers in a watering-hole and footprints in the mud reveal those drinks, or parts of ponds, which appeal most.

However, there's a drawback. Even with a few decoys out, you may discover that the birds would much rather drink somewhere else that day, ignoring you altogether. But you can play a trick on them that will give you a great day's sport. It's akin to covering in some holes when you're ferreting and haven't enough nets. All you do is blow up a few party balloons and tie one to the crossbar that is a characteristic of most cattle drinks. This'll spook any would-be drinkers. Use pink balloons, because then the woodies think there's a human face in every cattle drink – except one. Just make sure it's yours, and not the one in the fold of the hill that you have overlooked.

After harvesting, it doesn't take the woodies more than a few days to find all the spilt grain. Then, when the baling machine comes along and lifts the straw, more grain is revealed and it may not yet have sprouted if the harvest was early. But now that stubble burning and early ploughing are so popular, the birds soon have to retreat to the woods and partake of the harvest there. Beechmast (or nuts) and acorns are favourite, although this is the time when hawthorn berries are turning the bushes a dull scarlet, blazing strongly when the sun comes from behind a cloud. Elderberries appeal, too, and with so much food about it isn't easy to catch the birds out. However, afternoon walks ultimately reveal a copse where the birds can feed on hawthorn and elder and take a distant view of the world round about. A suitably-placed hide and a few decoys bring them back the next morning, expecting to feed. You should have an enjoyable day teaching them different.

Winter

As autumn fades into winter, so the woodland stalking improves, with woodies sharing the bag with squirrels and the odd rabbit on a day out. Late in the evening, before the weather turns really cold, I like to be out stalking through the bare woods. One of my favourite winter

shots was at a woodie that was sitting in the last of the sunshine, high in a birch tree. There were, in fact, about thirty woodies perched around a group of birches at the crown of a hill, inside a small wood. Soon after the sun dropped, they would make the short flight into a belt of thick conifers not more than a hundred yards away.

It had been a bitterly cold day, and the frost had started to wrinkle the edges of puddles beside the woodland path some hours before the sun set. The birds were gilded by the last rays, sitting huddled on the high wispy branches, their heads hunched into puffed-out breasts. It wouldn't take more than one of those drooping eyelids to flicker and catch a movement among the rhododendrons beneath. They were to be my passageway, if I was to get within range.

Patches of snow lingered on the woodland floor where the full strength of the sun had been unable to penetrate. I was careful to avoid them, lest a crunching footstep should catch a pigeon's ear. But the path was safe for a long way, so I could walk openly within a hundred yards. That was where the thick rhododendrons grew. They formed a barrier all around the birches, and I would have to slip through their intertwined branches like a weasel if I wasn't to send slides of snow crashing through the leaves and dusky stillness.

This was the major problem – not the chance of being spotted. I was in the gloom, wearing full camouflage, and was probably as invisible as I could ever be, unless I attracted attention. In my thermal clothing, I was sweating as each muscle strained to cope with changing contorted positions. It was impossible to do anything else if I was to climb over and crawl under the dense cover. Each branch had to be negotiated with a great deal of weaselling. But eventually I found the place I

135

wanted. One branch overhung another like a firing slot in a wartime concrete pillbox.

The birds, now so close, were still unaware of my presence. I looked through the scope at the nearest ones. All but one were screened behind a tracery of birch twigs. This one, though, was sitting more on my side of the tree and I had to move only a few inches to get a clear shot between two dangling twigs and straight into its heart. I had no need to hurry, as the birds were still hunched down like mops. This gave me the opportunity to get my breath and let my heartbeat settle. The bird was a long way off, slightly uphill and at the top of a tall tree. I decided to give it an inch, centred the cross-hairs on the top of its back, and softly tripped the trigger. The plop seemed so far away, but the pellet had found its mark. The pigeon was stone-dead before it smashed into the rhododendrons. It took a while to find, but it was worth persevering for – the pellet had dropped by as much as I'd expected and had taken the bird straight through the heart. It had been a most satisfying stalk with which to end a winter's day.

At other times the birds aren't nearly so helpful, though. Sometimes they all disappear for a while, leaving the woods empty until either a fresh batch arrives, or the originals return to the territory. Their movements are governed by food and weather to a large extent.

Where they roost is always dependent on the weather. Their favourite woods may not change, but they prefer to sleep in the least draughty part. Sometimes they sleep right down low in stormy weather, when the tree-tops are less appealing. You can have good sport like this, slipping through the woods on a dirty day, trying to spot the woodies before they notice you.

Feral and Racing Pigeons

Airgun hunters can also have good sport with feral pigeons. These are mongrels – mixtures of fantails, racing, blue rock, town and woodpigeons. They come in all colours and frequent cliffs and quarries, although they're not above camping out

The feral pigeon is fair game – just make sure it has no rings on its legs.

136

in ruined buildings and other places that you're bound to come across on your travels. If you take a shot at one against a cliff, reflect that if you miss, your shot will probably dislodge stones. Stand too close to the base, and they'll hit you in the face.

Never shoot any pigeon which you even remotely suspect of being a racer. Owners become very attached to their birds, and it could be like somebody shooting their pet dog. You can tell a racer because it's slightly smaller than a woodie and has an alert, fit look about it. The tell-tale sign is the ring on the leg. Sometimes racers go astray for a few days, and that's when you're likely to come across one. Generally it will be alone and show little sign of being alarmed. It is, after all, accustomed to human beings, and is even used to being driven hundreds of miles with masses of other birds in an articulated truck to a remote release point, possibly on the Continent.

Collared Doves

A visitor from the Continent started one of the biggest population explosions in the bird world for many a long year. Collared doves were sighted for the first in Britain about thirty years ago. They had spread from Turkey along the Mediterranean coast and northwards through Europe. In this brief span of years the species has proliferated throughout most of Britain.

Collared doves provide some interesting shooting. They haven't yet fully acquired the woodie's wariness of man, and this makes them fairly easy to approach. Indeed, the species offers shots that are much too easy. The birds sometimes appear to be intent on sitting on the end of your gun barrel. Once they wise up, they make much more challenging marks.

A collared dove eyes the farmyard from atop the barn roof.

Much of the technique for woodie shooting applies to collareds, too.

To my mind, though, the best time for hunting the collared dove is at harvest. Big flocks gather around barnyards where the grain and straw are being stored. A hide in the right place provides all the opportunities you can wish for – if you don't show yourself.

It's possible to decoy them, too. A few decoys on a tree overlooking a stubble field sometimes pulls in birds from all over the district. At other times of the year you have to take collared doves as you find them, and that's normally on the edge of woodland and farmland.

A dove that you once could shoot is the

137

Its crop stuffed with corn, a collared dove surveys the barnyard.

turtle dove, but it is now a protected species and is anyway too pretty by half to kill. When our paths cross, I leave it to go about its business undisturbed.

Cooking

After a good shoot at either woodies or collared doves – ferals, too, if you wish –

138

remove the breastbone for eating. This is much quicker than plucking, and barely wastes anything. All you do is slit the breast skin, peel it back to the wings which you cut away from the breastbone. You then put a finger under the sharp end and pull the whole thing away, complete with its two large flaps of muscle. This is the basis for many a fine dish. The meat can now be cooked without any hassle, using a wide range of recipes.

11 Corvids

The term corvid comes from the Latin name for the crow family. In the context of this book, it includes the magpie, jay, carrion crow, hooded crow, rook and jackdaw. I have a soft spot for jackdaws, they strike me as the most honest member of the tribe. They certainly have a cheerful chattering presence, whether they live among ruins, around cliffs, quarries, or in big old trees full of holes for them to nest in. I prefer to leave jackdaws to chatter among themselves.

The crow family has won itself the reputation of being the villains of the bird world. Cunning and handsome though they are, their interests clash with man's fondness for birds that sing sweetly or eat quaintly. The whole tribe are ruthless hunters and robbers of nests, eating fledglings or chicks without any hint of compassion. That's a human emotion, though, and not the type of thought that flashes through a predator's mind as it closes on its prey.

Nevertheless, some gamebirds, particularly grouse and grey partridges, are in such dire straits at the moment that they need every protection they can get. My personal reason for taking every opportunity to rid the world of corvids is that summer evenings filled with birdsong are a particular love of mine. Several times I've taken particular interest in nests in my garden, only to find a pair of forlorn parents hopping around the nest site. They'll remain confused like this for several hours — sometimes a day or two — unable to comprehend that their family has been borne aloft inside a magpie's gizzard.

My wish to hunt these birds is increased by the fact that they're very wary. This makes them worthy marks at any time. Usually they'll defeat you through their extreme suspicion of man. While they'll happily let innocent-looking people pass close by, they spot a man with a rifle from a long way off, and make themselves scarce. The instinct that preserves them is the same that saves the lives of bunnies — at the first hint of danger, they put as much space as possible between themselves and you. They don't hang around for a second look, though they'll drift overhead after being disturbed, dissecting the landscape beneath them with their sharp eyes. If you reveal yourself, your presence will be marked and they'll stay well away.

However, it's a known fact that crows can't count. A trick that gamekeepers use is for two people to walk up to where a carrion crow is nesting. One gets into position ready to shoot the hen when she returns to the nest, and possibly the cock bird too. The other person then walks back the way he came, tricking the birds into believing that the danger is over. *Bang!* It applies to all members of the group, allowing effective ambushes to be set in their favourite hang-outs.

The unpopularity of crows and magpies in particular, has grown in recent times through an increase in their numbers. Municipal rubbish tips and belts of thick conifers have provided crows with abundant food and shelter. Other factors are probably involved in the magpie's population explosion, but as yet they're

That most aristocratic of villains, the carrion crow, for all its cleverness offers airgun hunters a fairly easy target.

beyond my ken.

Neither this increase nor the damage that they do has gone unnoticed by farmers, keepers and landowners. This fact alone is likely to provide you with a chance of getting permission to shoot, particularly as few game shooters can be bothered to undertake any vermin control on their rented patch. Nevertheless, the crow family is ideal fare for the air rifle.

A silenced weapon is best, because it doesn't warn incoming corvids of the reception they're likely to receive. It's also perfect for use among rearing pens and so on. Show your host a few corpses at the

day's end and you'll be invited back for more. Convince everybody that you're OK and it won't be long before you're allowed a free hand to shoot woodies in the pheasant coverts and stalk rabbits on the hill.

Practically all members of the tribe, bar rooks and jackdaws perhaps, have an intense dislike for competition from other predators. They'll willingly tolerate each other, and even contribute to each other's mayhem. However, present them a hawk, owl or fox and they'll fling themselves into a fit of abuse. You can hear this quite often during walks in the woods – the screeching of jays, magpies, thrushes and blackbirds pin-pointing the place where a tawny or a barn owl has been caught out in the open.

You can readily cash in on this aggression by using a decoy owl. First you find a place where members of the gang spend most of the day. Build yourself a hide, but make sure it's invisible else you'll be hunted out by those sharp eyes once the shooting starts. The decoy needs to have bright yellow eyes. You can buy decoys of little owls. One make of these has flapping wings. If you tweak a string the wings flap, provoking the crows and magpies into a renewed frenzy of dive-bombing.

The eyes are important. They need to be threatening, and I have heard that a teddy bear with bright orange glass eyes can work wonders if nailed to a convenient post. Whatever type of decoy you use, remember that the rule is to make it look obvious, but natural. Therefore an owl pegged down in the middle of a field may not work as well as one on a fence post, or on a pole above the hedge.

Don't give yourself away by having to come out to pick off wounded birds. Shoot carefully, always remembering that a finishing-off shot should be ten times more precise than any other because, if you're normal, there'll be a hint of panic about it.

Once a few have been downed, you're likely to experience a thoroughly spooky episode that's straight out of Hitchcock's movie, *The Birds*. Magpies show a strong curiosity about their fallen brethren, but nothing like the frenzy that crows go into when they spot slain friends on the ground. They wheel around cawing loudly and raucously, swooping down beside the dead, often landing and squawking alongside them. The shooting potential of this situation is enormous. I'm not sure why it is – perhaps nothing more sinister than

Most of the crow family will mob a decoy owl. One with flapping wings will infuriate them even more.

curiosity. You can encourage it by leaving corpses pegged out near a hide; they're bound to attract attention.

Although I have never shot a hooded crow, I would imagine that this technique would apply to them as much as to carrion crows. Both types can be shot during the evening when they fly into woods. They have a special liking for the warmth

The author setting out a dead carrion crow as a decoy.

of thick conifers. This is excellent sport on the right evening, but you have to be careful with wind when roost shooting. Generally the preferred part of a wood is the downwind area, where birds can get a warm night's sleep without being thrashed about in their hammocks. On a still evening in winter, they flap and caw among the top branches of the beech trees before retiring to the firs for the night. You can have good sport, shooting from the gloom and keeping out of sight.

Even when roost shooting, it pays to leave your corpses so they can be seen — like out in the field on the edge of a wood. This will cause great scenes of wheeling and cawing, greatly increasing the bag, sometimes. It all depends on how wary they become, and whether their fixation with dead crows takes the upper hand.

Crows

Crows have become a speciality of mine, largely because they love using the tree at the bottom of my garden as a look-out point. It's also a desirable nesting site. The last one to fall to my rifle was sitting at the back of the tree, sheltering from a strong wind. The branches were flailing up and down, and the crow was riding his like it wasn't moving. Another branch was flapping between us. Most times it obscured the crow so effectively that no shot would make it through. Then, after watching for a couple of moments, I noticed that if the front branch went down and the crow's branch came up, its head and neck came clear in a small gap in the thick thatch of twigs. I stayed on aim, waiting. The breeze continued blowing, and the crow and the branches kept bobbing up and down. Then I noticed the rhythm changing again. The crow's head was about to reappear in that gap. I took careful aim on where it would happen and saw the whis-

The carrion crow – as wily a quarry as anybody could hope for.

kers on the crow's beak as it rose into the sight picture. Just before it stopped and took the down elevator, I squeezed. My timing, which had to be in milliseconds, was spot on. The crow slumped beneath its branch, hanging like a bat, its wings open. Then the nervous reaction weakened and it dropped like a stone.

Next morning, I placed it out in the vegetable garden and got two more that came swooping around, cawing raucously. In fact their tendency to announce their arrival in no uncertain terms is a blessing, I find. It enables me to go about

A carrion crow feeding its young from the carcass of a decoy rabbit.

my business without having to keep my eyes peeled, and just keeping the stereo turned down a bit. When the pirates arrive, I gather up the rifle from outside the door of my upstairs toilet and load it. Then open the door gingerly lest the movement be spotted, even through the frosted glass. I poke the tip of the silencer out of the fanlight window, and hope that this tiny movement isn't spotted, either. Often it is. If there aren't any crows at the top of that tree, it won't be long before there are. They alight, take a look around, and take off again after a few bellows at the decoy. They don't give much time, so each shot has to be quick and precise.

You have to be very careful when shooting out of a house lest you infringe the law by firing into other people's gardens. You also have to be careful, when firing through partially-open windows, that you don't shoot a chunk out of the frame. It happens. The best way to avoid splinters of lead ricocheting around the bathroom is either to poke the barrel clear, or make sure that you've compensated for the difference between the line of sight and the pellet's flight line. That's about two inches on my rig, at the point where the pellet emerges from the barrel. One or two nasty dents in my aluminium window frames testify to this difference.

Shooting out of the house is rather like firing from a permanent hide. It is all very convenient, but once it becomes identified as a potential source of danger, it will come under exacting scrutiny each time a crow comes near. I'm sure this is the reason why they now prefer to use the far side of my tree. They have learned the hard way, but I don't lack opportunities. Anyway, by reacting in this way, the crows have exposed a chink in their defence that I can exploit.

As a general principle, when a permanent hide becomes recognised and your quarry start to use a different part of a shelter belt, you can catch them completely by surprise by building another little cocoon where they're least expecting it. Mind you, too much pressure will cause them to decamp to more favourable sites.

In June, when the young carrion crows leave the nest, they sit for days on certain branches of specific trees where their parents can find them to feed them. Their constant puny cawing gives away their presence. If you wish to cull their numbers this is an easy time to thin the stock of crowlets.

Magpies

A method of decoying which works for crows, but is even more effective with magpies, is to stake a rabbit out in their territory and wait in a hide for the birds to come and check out the free meal. Repellent though it sounds, the most attractive bait is a bunny with its viscera hanging out. Magpies are partial to the eyes, so make sure you shoot them before they get to the delicacy. Otherwise the bait may prove to be less attractive.

Magpies are probably the most wary spivs of the crow family. They'll spot little movements in a hide which a carrion crow would never see. They are almost impossible to stalk. However, at the end of the summer you will often hear parties of them working through the woods, or maybe you'll find somewhere that they come to drink. If you hear them coming towards you, get into cover and wait for them to show. It can be quite exciting, especially if there are six or eight in the group.

Will they see you? Will they decide that another part of the woods holds more promise? No, here they come, flying low through the chestnut coppice. The first one comes even closer, and while it's flying you shoulder the rifle, ready for it to settle. As it perches on the lower branch of an oak, you're on to it, and it's tumbling almost before it can draw breath. Don't move. The crack of the rifle has silenced the 'pie family. Their chuckling has been replaced by silence as they drift deep into the cover. All you can hear now is the distant tractor buzzing in the field, gathering up the straw bales.

The family didn't miss the tumbling black and white mop, nor did they fail to mark the spot where it collapsed into last year's leaf litter. Right now, several pairs of beady eyes are scanning for signs of a movement. Pray that the cover and your stillness keep you hidden. There, away through the coppice greenery came a muted chuckle. Soon they'll start slipping back, with only the occasional muted little call to guide your eyes.

They'll come back by a different route, so keep scanning for that give-away flash

The magpie has such keen eyesight that it rarely misses the slightest suspicious movement.

The magpie is the wariest of the airgunner's quarry species.

of white. They're out there somewhere. With a soft *whoosh*, you hear the sound of wings close behind you. Freeze. Right now, from five yards away, a pair of sharp eyes is drilling into your back. Is it a tree stump? It's about the right colour and certainly not moving. With a chuckle, another 'pie flies to a twig about twenty-five yards to your left. It's more intent on its fallen friend than on you, so gently raise the rifle, hoping against hope that nothing goes wrong. *Crack!* You didn't spot that twig gently waving out of focus in the scope sight, and as the magpies flee, you look up to see it elegantly topple over, neatly shot through the middle.

Magpie families are fond of playing about close to water and sometimes you can set up a hide close by a woodland watering hole. You'll need to do a lot of creeping around until you discover these special places, they're not easy to find because few wild animals linger over their drinking. A flash or two of wings around a little pool where a fallen tree has dammed the stream is as good an indication as any that a hide would be worth setting. Look for signs of claw marks on the fallen trunk, where birds have walked down to the water's edge, or along the bank, if it isn't too steep.

This sort of ambush is likely to provide all sorts of surprises in wild woodland. You'll see squirrels, deer, foxes, wood-pigeons, and all sorts of birds dropping in for a drink. It's a good place to carry a camera, too, because of the opportunities. You would be surprised by the amount of wildlife that visits one of these watering-holes during a hot summer's day, especially when water supplies have been shrunk by drought.

Once, while I was out after magpies, a fox came and had a drink. It was sniffing around at a fallen magpie, when another swooped out of the trees and tweaked the fox's tail. It instantly hopped out of striking range. The fox turned around, glared at it, and turned back to the dead magpie. He picked it up and the other bounced back in for another tweak. The fox pretended to jump at it, and the bird fled into a low bush. As Mr Reynolds trotted off into cover, I persuaded the other to take the place of its departed friend. Since then, I've been told by other countrymen that magpies have a weakness for annoying foxes this way. At other times they mob them more vocally.

Because magpies scavenge so variously, it isn't easy to locate a favourite source of food to mount an ambush near. Yet they do have their favourite trees – the big thorn-bush in the middle of a hedgerow is a classic. There'll probably be a nest there, too.

In October, you can ambush magpies in meadows and paddocks where they chase daddy-long-legs. Their antics are quite comical as they chase the gangly flies over the grass, fluttering, hopping and bouncing in pursuit. From your hide in the hedge you will often be hard pressed not to laugh at it all. But the magpies are working closer to you, four of them, with another group in the far corner of the field. Wait until they're well within range, then shoot. Once again, if you don't show yourself, they may come back to investigate. But there are times when a dead magpie is an effective scarer, too, and you could discover that your first shot was the last, with the 'pies preferring to chase daddies up in the far corner. A removal job may be in order.

You can also attract magpies by calling them. All you need is a half-full household-size box of matches which you rattle. The secret is to listen to the magpies, then imitate them. Notice the short six-note chuckle, then the single clucks, all of which can be reproduced quite easily with a matchbox. Note also the tempo of their calls. Just because they don't answer you doesn't mean that they haven't heard you. However, you can overdo the calling and drive them away. They might think that you're a demented relative and therefore best avoided.

Jays

Jays have a passion for acorns which they share with woodpigeons. I've spent many pleasant hours in autumn oak woods, sniping at the jays as they flit through the uppermost branches. Once most of the acorns have fallen, they join the woodies in shuffling through the carpet of dead leaves beneath the trees. Some oaks produce tastier fruit than others, it would appear, because often a specific tree receives much more attention, even though others in the same group are all fruiting.

Jays are unusual in that they stash away acorns and beechmast for harsh times much like squirrels. In winter you'll find groups of jays working the leaf litter under beech and oak trees. They are hunting their buried treasures, and other titbits revealed by harsh winds blowing away the cover of dead leaves.

Jays are quick-witted, quick-moving birds. They prefer to linger deep in woodland or to forage close to the edge, rarely far from cover. Often you'll hear unseen birds screeching from deep inside the wood, even when they are not alarmed. Shots are presented quite by chance most of the time, so unless you find something that draws and concentrates the birds, you will just have to hope that your paths cross. They like to check out farmyards and gardens on occasion, even though they're most wary of man. This is hardly surprising because the jay's blue-barred wing feathers are prized by fishermen for tying flies for sea trout. A bunch of these waxy strands is essential on many different fly patterns.

I think the jay can be considered by most shooters as a rare prize because it spends so much time in deep cover, marking the least sign of intrusion. Luck plays an enormous part in the shooting of one. When you accomplish it, one of those barred feathers in your hat should be a suitable memento of the encounter.

Rooks

Rooks have a mixed reputation with farmers. Although they do a great deal of good by eating wire-worms and leather jackets out in the pastures, they aren't above stealing either crops or baby birds. This makes them less popular.

There also is a traditional reason for shooting them – rook pie. On or close to 12 May each year, the young birds leave the nest. It is possible to shoot them inside the nest, but such conduct is totally unbecoming of a sportsman. With a bit of luck, on a fine morning you'll find the topmost branches of the ash trees spotted by flapping young rooks.

Besides keeping their numbers in check, this traditional type of shooting provides the young squabs which go inside the pie. It's not easy shooting, either, because they flutter around the tree-tops that are themselves rocking gently in the breeze. As they're often so high up, you'll be challenged by some tricky marksmanship, but then that's what shooting with air rifles is all about. When it's all over, take your slain and gently cut the skin down the breast. Peel away the skin, then cut away the wings and lift out the entire, meat covered breastbone. The foxes will collect the spare parts the next evening, while you're breaking the crust of that savoury pie.

It is important to be fully camouflaged and to make your presence as unobtrusive as possible, if you want the adult birds to return while all this shooting is going on. At the first few shots they'll be off to a distant belt of trees, from which to observe their rookery. Occasionally, because silenced rifles merely spit, a scout will feel confident enough to drift over, high above the branches. Let it go because it may bring back the others. In the meantime, though, the disturbance causes other squabs to take to the twigs, presenting more opportunities as the morning wears on.

The date when the rooks fly seems to have little to do with the weather; although a severe spring may delay them by a day or three, but certainly little more. Around my part of the world 12 May is when they fly; in cooler northerly parts of Britain, they fly a day or so later.

With rooks so partial to the open fields, it isn't easy to get close enough to shoot them for much of the rest of the year. You can ambush them, like crows, among their roosting trees. Sometimes they show a keen interest in places where cattle feed is scattered, or around feed troughs. These are good opportunities for ambushing – maybe a stalk or two.

Personally I don't feel vindictive towards rooks. The annual squab shoot is about as much as my conscience can take in this department. Even though opportunities present themselves quite often when I'm out shooting, I prefer to leave the survivors to add their distinctive character to the countryside. The fields would be empty without rooks – they're always worth watching because their social behaviour is so interesting.

12 Field Target Shooting

I was involved with the first ever field target shoot. That was back in September 1980, on a glorious day of sunshine in the field behind the Red Lion at Magham Down. Yet I'm sure that none of us that day had any idea that the practice would become so popular so quickly. It showed that the sport of shooting with air rifles needed a boost like this, an extra dimension that has undoubtedly increased its popularity at all levels.

The full consequences have yet to be felt, although you can read the signs in the number of fine looking, custom-built rifles that are for sale nowadays. As the sport becomes more popular, so the demands for smooth power and absolute accuracy are bound to increase. This is gradually improving the performance of all air weapons.

Performance, that's the name of the game – being able to zap any target, under any conditions, at any range – sometimes against the clock. And all for the highest motives – prestige and money. These catalysts have given us a thousand and one different championships in almost as many sports. Whatever the motives, the urge is there to shoot as perfectly as possible. No doubt the top scorers could teach me a trick or two about accuracy that would prove valuable out on the hill.

The secret to super-accurate shooting is super-familiarity with your rig and how it shoots. This comes to everybody in time, although some people have to practise longer and harder to compensate for a lesser degree of natural ability. It all depends on how much you want it.

If you're going to win, you'll need a positive mental attitude. Go for it. Without this you'll never make the grade. A lot of travelling around the country is required to get to the various shoots. It's all very well to be a crack shot on the home range, but you still might go to pieces in a major shoot. Every shot counts, and such factors as gamesmanship, the muttering crowd, the weather, and your mind can all affect your performance on the day, just as much as how well your rifle is shooting.

Precision and Consistency

At the outset, it's hard to appreciate just how much precision you'll have to instil into yourself if you're to win confidently under pressure. The accuracy of the top guys will already have caught your attention, yet you detect scant difference between their technique and yours. But it's there, it's known as experience, and it comes only after hard graft and no small degree of disappointment.

Precision starts with the basic outfit. Most field target shooters prefer to shoot .177 because of its flat trajectory just under the legal power limit. This means that sighting adjustments are not particularly excessive at the different ranges. The

Sign of the times at The Game Fair, testimony to the great increase in interest in air weapons.

pellets, however, tend to be on the heavier side because some of the catches on field targets are stiff. Sometimes the release-plate is so stiff that only a heavy smack in the middle will trip it. The slightly heavier pellet carries more clout, but avoids the .22's droopy flight pattern.

Consistent power is of paramount importance, and shooters keep their rifles in the cool during hot weather lest lubricants creep in the heat and push the power over the legal limit. If your rifle fails the chronograph test at the start of the range, you won't be allowed to shoot. Such erratic performance is now precluded from the top makes of rifle during the design stage.

Consistent performance ensures a consistent trajectory for the pellet. This is vital. It is a thread of certainty from which to weave victory. But a pellet's flight pattern is affected not just by power and calibre, but by the weight and size of each pellet. These two factors affect the relationship each shot has with the inside of your barrel. They too must be kept consistent for maximum precision.

Practically all of the top field target shooters weigh and size their pellets, rejecting piles of them because they fail these two simple tests. The ones that pass are then stored and loaded very carefully to prevent any distortion. However, when I'm out hunting the hills and valleys,

The knock-down design of target has revolutionised air rifle shooting as a sport.

I'm much more effective if I have a pocketful of pellets to grab at, and the rattling around makes a nonsense of weighing and sizing.

With consistency of performance so critical, most shooters prefer the sitting position, altering only their point of aim or adjusting the scope between shots. Don't overlook the increasingly popular lucky cushion – and why not? Just make sure yours has a waterproof cover. It often rains at field shoots.

About the worst thing you can do is to spend hours on the sighting range fiddling with your scope. If you're shooting a half-decent rig, it'll hold a perfect zero at all times. By all means use the range to warm up on. It'll give you extra confidence on the day to know that you and your rig can zap anything with a string attached.

The Shoot

Start by getting the most reliable weather forecast you can find for where the shoot is being held. If storms are expected later, make sure you shoot before they arrive. Get there early. This allows you to unwind after the journey and to become familiar with the layout. Make a careful note of where the organisers have included tricks and special problems for you to solve. Watch for the glade on the far side of trees where a wind is gusting. These points become second nature after a season or two. The performance of other shooters soon reveals the targets which will require you to take extra care before slipping the shot.

Over one hundred and twenty field target clubs have sprung up since that first shoot in 1980 with more starting up as interest mushrooms. Several clubs already have more than a hundred members. This is an excellent state of affairs, and of permanent value to the sport. Air rifle shooting has gained a respectable, formal representation at last – like that of clay pigeon shooting.

The sport has become so popular in recent years that the sheer weight of competitors is forcing the sport to try to regulate itself. However, with its roots still firmly embedded in wild open places, shooters are unwilling to see too much formality creeping in. Some think that it's already bad enough having crows which fall down with a loud clang when you shoot them.

Some of the big open shoots in the annual calendar attract long queues of competitors. It's probable that the sport will avail itself of some of the clay pigeon shooters regulation book, and limit the queues by sending squads through the layout, with each starting at a specific time.

One very unnatural element is the time that competitors take to fire each shot.

The psychological pressures on the firing line at a major shoot are different from any you'll ever find in wild places.

On the field target circuit, a light-shielding hat permits the clearest sight picture.

Some take ages, and that's generally not possible with most wild animals. If a premium was placed on time taken, shoot-offs at the day's end could be prevented.

Another more realistic trick would be a rabbit target sited behind a tangle of wire, requiring competitors to shoot through it in the standing position, for example. Tricks like these can attract premium points in the event of a tie, and prevent the need for a shoot-off. Some clubs already run this idea.

The secret of a successful shoot is that the layout should be varied, using up-in-tree sites, dips, bushes and all of the available natural ground cover for the targets. Long-range targets should be limited because good shooters can hit them without trouble – they only slow them down. One sited thirty yards away in the roots of a tree could be tougher for shooters to hit.

Course organisers who create layouts filled with variety will find shooters discussing the problems involved and taking an interest in how their friends are shooting. This makes the event much more cohesive for everybody. Tricky targets are preferable to ones at excessively long ranges because they're more rewarding for beginners. The idea is to send competitors home happy at hitting quite a few, sad that they didn't manage to hit too many, but satisfied. Nobody benefits if only the top shots can hit anything.

One element that troubles me is that the rifles being used by some top competitors are edging further and further away from the weapons that founded the sport. During the early years, if you wanted a swift appraisal of every hunting rifle on the market, you had only to go to a field target shoot and you'd see it in action, and maybe could borrow it for a few shots on the zeroing range. Nowadays they all seem to be Weihrauch HW77 clones. Many of these customised weapons have borrowed chunks of design from target rifles – hooked butts, adjustable cheek-pieces and complex innards. Soon they'll be recoilless and the sport will lose the distinct contrast that it has with paper punching. But how does one curb this elitist trend without sapping the initiative which pushes rifle design towards ever greater standards of excellence?

Organisation

The sport has a governing body that is trying to formulate rules that will retain the air of relaxed informality while providing some sort of a framework for it to grow on. The British Field Target Council has adopted a standard kill area of 45mm (1.75inches) on knock-down targets. Nevertheless, its rule book is nothing like that of the Clay Pigeon Shooting Association.

Chronographing is starting to become standardised. Organisers have wised up to shooters who load with tight-fitting or heavy pellets for the test, then revert to lighter, zippier, illegal ammunition for the main event. They'll have to get wise to all sorts of things before the next decade is out.

There can be little doubt that the sport is poised to take off in a big way –

Practically any design of field target is permitted in shoots, provided the kill area measures 45mm wide – and it falls flat when hit.

probably even unto the realm of television. Already international competitions have been shot and won, by crack British teams.

The significance of a sport being organised at club and national level becomes apparent when standards need to be set and when political muscle is required to ensure that new laws are seen to be fair to everybody taking part. Air rifles are frequently threatened with additional curbs of legislation, and extra political clout goes a long way towards moderating the notions of civil servants.

I originally planned to include a list of field target clubs in this book. However, with interest increasing year by year, such a list would be out of date before you could read it. Moreover, it is the nature of

First-class facilities in the woods at a top field target club's private layout.

clubs that one guy does all the work while the rest enjoy the facilities. So addresses would change because field target clubs have the habit of splitting, with part of the original contingent going off and creating their own club ground somewhere else.

Your best bet, though, would be to consult with air rifle dealers in your area. They'll tell you what's what, and who you might be advised to steer clear of. Some of these clubs are a bit exclusive, with every miss being discussed right down to the last grain of lead. Club experience at this level is essential, though, because the more intense the competition that exists between club members, the higher their average scores will be. Although the tuition is likely to be excellent at such clubs – an excellent reason for joining – you might become demoralised if you start off there.

An increasing number of open club matches are held around Britain throughout the summer, together with events at country fairs. Few of these can even hope to match the excellent courses that are laid out at the Game Fair. These events provide field target facilities to shooters who haven't a club near home.

The alternative is to start your own. This requires investment in knock-down targets to begin with, although many clubs seem to have a member who's a dab hand at metal working. I'm surprised that there aren't more indoor field target clubs in large towns because there are ample facilities for them. Every evening, after offices close down, a huge acreage of underground car-parking space becomes available. At weekends, they remain cold, silent and empty. There could never be a safer place to shoot, so all you who work in big office blocks should get your act together.

Richard Welham in action. Regular winners leave nothing to chance,
so winning weapons are starting to look like match rifles.

Underground car-parks have bare concrete walls that shatter most pellets. If ricochets prove to be a problem, though, a more absorbent backdrop should be substituted. Obviously it is impossible to nail targets to the ground, so an alternative means of attachment has to be found – like mounting them on a heavy metal plate. It'll help, too, if the knock-downs don't require a hefty tug to reset them.

All range markings can be done with thick felt tip on the concrete, permitting a permanent record of what goes where when you come to set up. A lucky cushion keeps oil smudges off your best office suit. Why don't you suggest the idea to your Managing Director now, this minute. After all, you've got nothing else to do now that you've finished reading my book...

Good shooting!

Index